THE MUSICAL TEACHER

Preparing Teachers to Use Music in the Childhood Classroom

Jinyoung Kim
College of Staten Island

KENDALL/HUNT PUBLISHING COMPANY
4050 Westmark Drive   Dubuque, Iowa 52002

Jinyoung Kim is assistant professor and a coordinator of the early childhood education program at College of Staten Island, the City University of New York, where she teaches music in childhood. Previously she taught in pre-K setting in both Seoul, Korea and NYC. She received her M.A. and Ed. D from Teachers College, Columbia University. She has published several articles and books about children's music and music integration. Her composition of children's songs was published in Korean and she won runners-up for her song 'Never Ending Melody' at John Lennon Songwriting Contest in 2002.

Cover image from Digital Vision.

Copyright © 2004 by Jinyoung Kim

ISBN 13: 978-0-7575-1476-0
ISBN 10: 0-7575-1476-6

Printed in the United States of America
10 9 8 7 6 5 4 3 2

Contents

[Musical Planning and Classroom Teachers]

Dedicated to

My Father in Heaven

Who...
Is the Main Source of Knowledge
Made the World by His Word
Knows Everything of What He Made
And Teaches His Knowledge and His Wisdom

Who...
Is the Potter with Skillful Hands
Has Made All Things
Molded Me in His Image
And Teaches His Ways

Who...
Is the Composer of Love Songs
Feels My Heart
Cares for Me with His Heart
And will be Glorified with the Song of Praises.

Preface

We live in a world flooded with information where with one click of a mouse, we can access thousands of related articles and websites regarding specific subjects. In this world, how can we filter floods of information to make meaningful knowledge to satisfy the needs of teachers as well as students?

Teaching music to college students in the program of early childhood and elementary education, I have come to understand various needs for teaching candidates even before they teach their own students. Their musical background and experiences are so different from each other. Some may be able to read musical notes, while others have no musical knowledge at all. Some of them have taken music lessons, while others have never played a musical instrument.

The educational setting they will confront as classroom teachers may be even more diverse. Some schools may have abundant resources: musical instruments, recordings, and other music-related materials, while others may not have enough in their budgets for music. A small number of schools may have music specialists who visit the school once or twice a week and teach children music, while most expect classroom teachers to integrate all subjects. The children they will meet are also different from each other in their development, ability, cultural background, and musical experiences.

To reflect diversity, ways of teaching must be different from one another. Teacher education can no longer prepare teachers by transmitting knowledge and giving ready-made teaching materials. Teachers in contemporary education need to be reflective practitioners with the abilities of critical thinking and creative planning so that they can apply their knowledge into their own practice of teaching.

Sharing the burden of teacher educators and knowing a book cannot satisfy all the needs of pre and in-service teachers, I feel obligated to describe what this book doesn't have, as well as what does.

First, this book contains *knowledge*. However, it does not always provide all the information. In writing this book, I use an activity-based format, hoping that readers do not just accumulate informational knowledge. At the same time, I want readers to construct knowledge while participating in activities. Teachers should be able to search for useful and appropriate information, select and construct knowledge, and transfer select information into comprehensible knowledge not only for themselves, but for the children they teach. Through this process, they can build up Practical Theory.

Second, this book contains *skills*. However, this is not an activity book with teaching materials we often get from workshops. As mentioned earlier, teachers' musical background and teaching skills, children's individual differences, and educational settings are diverse. Teachers cannot depend only on ready-made materials that give one direction for all. Teachers need to develop their teaching skills as well as music skills so that they can develop musical activities appropriate for their students, making creative teaching materials as needed. Through this process, they will develop Theoretical Practice.

Third, this book contains *dispositional experiences*. It is not a book of philosophy or edification. I do not want teachers to go into educational settings feeling uncomfortable with teaching music, carrying all the burdens in the name of "what teachers should do" or "what is for the children." If so, they will fall into the trap asking children to appreciate what they can't enjoy. Similar to listening to music in a car or singing in the shower, I want teachers to enjoy the music when they integrate it with other areas of the curriculum. To do so, I want users of this book to share their feelings as they go through the process of understanding knowledge, developing skills, and gaining music appreciation. Through this process they will become Reflective Practitioners.

This book was written based on practical research in my classes Music in Early Childhood and Music in Elementary Education, taught in the last six years. These classes are designed for pre-service teachers in early childhood and elementary education who will become classroom teachers. This successful research proved my belief that education is not to catch fish for students but to teach them how to catch fish for themselves, and I have become convinced that classroom teachers will be able to create their own curriculum, integrating music for their own class.

I wish to acknowledge the contribution of my colleagues in the department of education who have stimulated my thinking and given meaningful input. Thanks to Susan Sullivan who has encouraged my professional growth and reviewed the text with her critical analysis and valuable suggestions.

Jinyoung Kim, Ed.D
Department of Education
The College of Staten Island, City University of New York

Unit 0: Introduction

Introduction
*

Explanation of the structure of each unit

.

What to learn and how to utilize this book

Unit 0
Introduction

You will learn and reflect on music and teaching through:

0-1.   Building Knowledge

0-2.   Developing Skills

0-3.   Experiencing

0[*]-1. Building Knowledge

Activity 0-1-(1)

1. Activities 0-1 will help you learn and understand musical knowledge such as musical concepts in different ways.
    - The purpose of this activity is to help you:
    - Search for music and/or teaching related concepts
    - Make music related information your own knowledge
    - Think about how to explain the words to children in developmentally appropriate ways

    - The activities include:
    - A scientific experiment to learn musical concepts
    - A brainstorming process to explain (or let the children explore) musical concepts

2. In Activity 0-1, you will have an opportunity to search for knowledge you will need to teach children.
    - The research will include different areas such as:
    - Children's musical development
    - Music teaching methods and/or activities
    - Developmentally appropriate teaching materials

    - You can search and share some useful resources such as:
    - Web sites: to get knowledge, teaching methods, etc. (Not always accurate)
    - Literature, journal articles, etc. (Users of this book can always update information as needed.)

    - You will need to organize the information.
    - You can use the information in an appropriate way to organize your knowledge.
    - To organize knowledge, you will be able to use different formats such as charts, tables, and other helpful tools.

---

* The number '0' has been used to represent each unit.

0-2. Developing Skills

Activity 0-2-(1)

1. In Activity 0-2, you will be participating in some musical activities.
    - These activities are:
      - Hands-on activities to learn musical concepts
      - Activities to integrate musical concepts into the curriculum.

    - These activities will help you:
      - Learn musical concepts by doing
      - Think about what you would do with children

2. In 0-2, you will also have an opportunity to share your ideas and discuss issues.
    - You can develop your skills of planning music activities. For example, you will be asked to:
      - Think of how to apply the same activity into activities for children in different developmental levels.
      - Find different ways of integrating musical concepts into the curriculum.

    - You will share your ideas with your classmates.
      - Encourage each other to come up with good ideas.
      - Build up each other's ideas.

0-3. Experiencing

Activity 0-3-(1)

1. You will be participating in other types of activities in Activity 0-3.
   - You will be asked to:
   - Listen to the music
   - Play music in a group
   - Etc.

   - The activities will help you:
   - Feel the music through listening, playing, dancing, and creating.
   - Appreciate music before teaching.

2. You will be asked to discuss music and/or teaching-related issues.
   - The discussion is to help you express your thoughts and feelings on:
   - Your teaching efficacy
   - Your educational philosophy
   - etc.

Reflection on Unit 0

At the end of each unit, you will write a reflective journal about what you've felt:

1. In the process of learning, searching, and getting knowledge

2. In the process of doing, planning, creating activities and developing your skills

3. In the process of listening, moving to, singing, playing, and creating music

Unit 1: Sound and Timbre

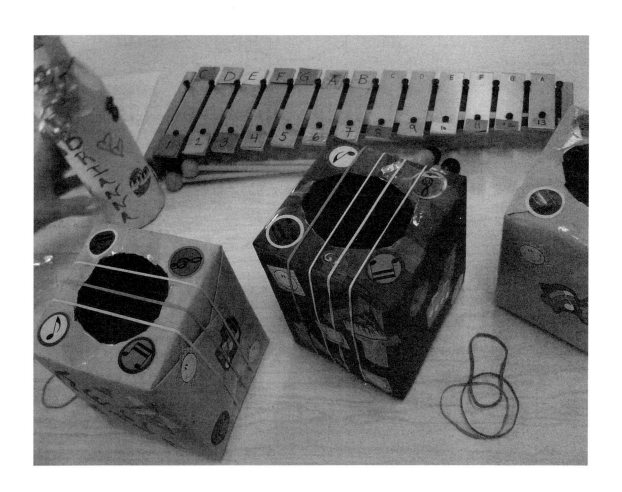

Sound
*

The stimulation of the auditory nerves
by vibrations carried in the air.

.

It is any motion
that breaks silence
and is detected through hearing.

.

It may be a noise,
or a pleasant musical sound.

Timbre
Tone Color
*

The character of a sound

.

It refers to the quality of sound that distinguishes
one musical instrument from another

Unit 1
Sound and Timbre

You will learn and reflect on music and teaching through:

1-1. Building Knowledge

1-1-(1) Sound
1-1-(2) Timbre

1-2. Developing Skills

1-2-(1) Sounds of Environment and Nature
1-2-(2) Sounds of Body and Voice
1-2-(3) Sounds of Objects and Musical Instruments

1-3. Experiencing

1-3-(1) Cultural Sounds
1-3-(2) Timbre in Music

1-1. Building Knowledge
1-1-(1) Sound

Activity 1-1-(1)

---

1. Define the sound in your own words. *a noise, vocal utterance or musical tone that causes an audible effect.*

2. Discuss different ways to explore sound.
    - Think about how we can hear sound. What are the ways you can see vibration made by sound? For example:
        - Say 'Ah ---'and touch your neck to feel the vibration of vocal muscles on your neck.
        - Make sounds into a microphone and observe the wave of your voice in the monitor.
        - My idea: *let air out of an inflated balloon and feel vibration + noise of air escaping*
    - Think of some ideas on how sound can make a vibration. For example,
        - Fill a glass of water. Bang a pan next to it and observe the wave of water.
        - My idea: *Put your hand on a speaker as music is playing*
    - Brainstorm the sounds we can hear.
        - You can hear now: Somebody talking, Air-conditioning, etc.
        - What you could hear if you go outside: Wind blowing, bird chirping, wave of ocean, people walking, etc.
        - What I can hear: *television, fan, typing on keyboard*

3. Put sounds into a certain category.
    - Put sounds you wrote above into sound-family groups and name each group. For instance:
        - You can categorize the sound based on where you hear it or how it was made.
        - Sounds can be categorized in terms of subjects that make each sound different such as human sound, animal sound, or machine sounds
        - My category of sound sources:

    - Think about some other ways to categorize sound.
        - Example:
        High / medium / low sounds

        Transportation
        Animal sounds

[Table 1-1] Sound Sources

Category	Sources	Sound Example
The Sound-Out *(The sound is given from outside. I can hardly control the sound but hear it depending on where I am.)*	Environment	Car honking, wind blowing, people talking, birds + animals, clock ticking, alarm
	Nature	Raindrops, wind, storm, birds, animals, dog barking, crickets waves breaking
The Sound-In *(The sound is in me so I carry the potential sound. I make the sound when I need to.)*	Body	Clapping, stamping knuckles cracking
	Mouth/Voice	Whistling, singing laughing, humming snoring
The Sound-With *(I can make the sound when I play it.)*	Objects	Blow dryer, Washing machine, air conditioner, fan, ~~lights~~
	Musical Instruments	Drum, tambourine, flute, piano

- My category of sound sources:

High / low —

1-1. Building Knowledge
1-1-(2) Timbre

Activity 1-1-(2)

1. Define timbre.
   - Research the definition from a music dictionary.[1]
   - The quality of sound that distinguishes one musical instrument from another instrument[2]
   - My search: *The characteristic quality of a sound, independent of pitch and loudness, from which its source or manner of production can be inferred. — Tone color.*
   - Define in your own words. For example:
   - The unique sound of musical instruments.
   - My definition: *The distinctive quality of sound by an instrument independent of pitch and loudness*

2. Learn about musical instruments.
   - Find resources from which you can get the knowledge about musical instruments. For example:
   - Websites[3] that have description and sound of each musical instrument
   - Catalogue or websites of music company[4]
   - CD, Books, Videotapes, etc.
   - My resources: *Music store - talking to owner or musicians*

   - Learn about musical instruments in different ways. For example:
   - Know the name, sound, and figures of each instrument
   - Describe the sound of each instrument in different words, colors, etc.
   - See if a certain sound of a musical instrument reminds you of any other image or sound

   4 groups
   - Put musical instruments into one of four family groups.
   - <u>Percussion</u>: bang, shake, or scrape.
   - <u>String</u>: pluck, stroke, or use a bow
   - <u>Wind-blown (Woodwind and Brass)</u>: blow
   - <u>Keyboard</u>: press keys

   - Fill in the following table with musical instruments you've researched (Table 1-1-(2) on the next page).

---

[1] The same musical term can be defined in different words in different dictionaries.
[2] Randel, D. M. (ed.). (1986). *The New Harvard Dictionary of Music*. MA: The Belknap Press of Harvard University Press
[3] http://www.lehigh.edu/zoellner/encyclopedia.html
[4] http://www.musicmotion.com; http://www.suzukimusic.com; http://www.westmusic.com; http://www.yamaha.com

[Table 1-1-(2)] Musical Instruments

Type	How to play	Musical Instruments
Percussion	Bang	Claves Cymbals *Rhythm sticks*
	Shake	Castanets Maracas
	Scrape	Guiro Cabasa *glockenspiel (metal)* *castanets* *handbell* *Triangle, timpani,* My research: *gong, drums, xylophone (wood)* *tic toc block, sandpaper blocks*
String	Pluck, stroke, use a bow	Violin Guitar *Double bass,* My research: *banjo, harp, cello* *harp, viola*
Wind-blown (Woodwind + Brass)	Blow *brass:- trombone, trumpet, tuba, horn*	Oboe Harmonica *Flute, bassoon, oboe* My research: *clarinet, recorder, harmonica, saxophone*
Keyboard	Press keys	Piano Electric keyboard *organ, accordian* My research: *harpsichord*

1-2. Developing Skills
1-2-(1) Sounds of Environment and Nature

Activity 1-2-(1)

---

1. Explore the sounds of our environment and/or nature.
   - Select a place to sit for 10 minutes. For example,
     - A subway station, playground, your apartment, or a cafeteria
     - The place I chose: *My Living room.*

   - Sit quietly and record all the sounds you hear. For instance, you can:
     - Record the sound using a record player.
     - Write about the sound you hear.
     - Draw
     - My record: *Typing on computer, sounds of the dishwasher (water + clicking) Fan, Talking in another room, traffic outside, children playing outside, refrigerator in kitchen.*
   - Bring what you recorded to the class.
     - Share what you recorded
     - What did you learn during the process of the activity? *There are many background sounds that occur that we do not notice unless we are making a conscious effort to listen*

2. Discuss musical activities for children.
   - Considering children's developmental level, what kind of activities can you do with children? For example:
     - Field trip: going for sound exploration
     - Sound hunting: Using a simple recording device, the children can catch and record sounds of the environment.
     - My idea: *Chart with pictures, have children go on a listening walk + mark off the pictures of the things they hear.*
   - How can we develop classroom activities?
     - In the listening center, the recorded sound along with picture cards can be provided so that the children can match the picture with the sound.
     - Listening to the sound recorded from the field trip, and have the children imitate the sound with their voice or other objects.
     - My idea: *Use nature sounds tapes - often relaxation tapes - at rest time and have children try to picture the scene with their eyes closed while resting. eg bird sounds, water*

1-2. Developing Skills
1-2-(2) Sounds of Body and Voice

Activity 1-2-(2)

1. Make musical sounds using your body and/or voice.
   - You can work in small groups of four to six people.

   - Each group can make a decision on what kind of sound they will make. For example:
     - Sounds made only using hands
     - Sounds made with mouth or using voices
     - Sounds made with any body part
     - Combination of above
     - Our group made: *clapping, snapping & humming sounds.*

   - Each group member makes different sounds. For example:
     - Clap twice.
     - Tap soft and getting louder.
     - My sound: *clapping.*

   - Make a plan sheet to arrange each member's sound-playing. For example:
     - Each sound can be played one after another or together.
     - You can repeat the same sound.
     - My group's sound arrangement: *We each played a rhythm + hummed a melody to it.*

2. Have a small concert to present each group's performance
   - Record each group's performance.

   - When all the performances are finished, play back the recorded performance.

   - Share your impression on the performance. For instance:
     - How did you feel being a member of the performance?
     - How was the recorded version of sound? Any difference?
     - My impression on the recorded performance: *When playing it is uplifting to work in a team on a rhythmical piece.*

3. Create an activity you can do with the children. *Ask children to brainstorm different ways to use their body parts to make sound. Have them demonstrate to the class + have the class try to follow. Try to play their "instruments" to a simple melody.*

1-2. Developing Skills
1-2-(3) Sounds of Objects and Musical Instruments

Activity 1-2-(3)

1. Exploring sound with objects.
   - Bring in an object with which you can make sound. The object does not have to be a musical instrument. The object can be something you find in your environment. For example:
     - Hair drier, kitchen utensils such as spoons, etc.
     - What I brought: *A small squaretin (tea box) with a lid.*
   - Make 3 different sounds with the object you brought.
     Put an object inside + shake. Hit like a drum – run a pencil around the inside
   - Share your ideas about the relationship between the sounds you heard or made with the object and musical instruments. For example:
     - What musical instrument it reminds you of
     - Ways of playing.
     The sounds were like a maraca + drum.

2. Think about activities to make musical instruments with children.
   - Think about what kind of musical instruments children can make with recycled materials. For example:
     - <u>Drum</u>: Different containers or cans covering the top with different types of materials such as oil-paper, etc.
     - <u>Maraca</u>: Put different amounts or types of materials in different bottles or other containers.
     - <u>Tambourine</u>: Using a plastic plate, hang different materials such as clips, bells, macaroni, etc.
     - <u>Ocean Drum</u>: Put beans, marbles, or so forth, into flat and wide containers such as a pizza box.
     - More ideas:

   - Develop some questions to encourage children to explore different sounds while they are making musical instruments.
     - How can you make different sounds?
     - Will it be different if you use different containers?
     - Does it make a difference if you put more or less grains in? Why?
     - How can you play it? Is there any other way to play it?
     - What does it sound like? Does it remind you of other sounds?
     - More ideas:
     Does it make a loud or quiet sound? How could you make it louder or quieter? Would it make a different sound if the materials you use on the outside or inside are different?

1-3. Experiencing
1-3-(1) Cultural Sound

Activity 1-3-(1)

---

1. Listen to the music played by traditional musical instruments from other cultures
   - Listen to and feel the sound of different cultures.
   - My feeling:

   - Research traditional musical instruments of other countries.
   - Pictures and/or recordings[1].
   - Videotapes such as the people from other cultures playing traditional musical instruments[2].
     Internet — CDROM - Music of the Peoples of the World
   - What kind of questions can you ask to help children's exploration?
   - How do those instruments look?
   - What do they sound like?
   - What are the similarities and differences, compared to the musical instruments you already know?

2. Discuss some issues regarding multicultural education and music.
   - Why do you think it is important for children to experience the music from different cultures? For example:
   - To learn: to know similarities, differences, and diversity.
   - To understand: to accept others
   - To communicate & share: to live together
   - My thoughts: *to hear music from other countries is an intrinsic way to understand the culture of the country.*
   - What are limitations or misconceptions we can have in multicultural education?

   Misconcep: That music from other countries may not be understood or liked by the children. That there is no difference so why play music from other countries when there is such a wide variety of music from here.
   Limitations! = children may not always be able to see what kind of instrument that is playing the music.

---

[1] http://www.brazilianpercussion.com;
[2] *The JVC Video Anthology of World Music and Dance.* Cambridge, MA: A Production of JVC, Victor Company of Japan, Ltd.

1-3. Experiencing
1-3-(2). Timbre in Music

Activity 1-3-(2)

1. Listen to and feel the music of different musical instruments.
   - What should we consider in planning and selecting music for children to explore timbre? For example:
   - Musical instruments from different groups such as percussion, keyboard, wind-blown (woodwind/brass), and string
   - Musical recordings in which the sound of one musical instrument stands out.
   - Music should not be too long or heavy for children to listen to.
   - My thoughts: *Music from different cultures is a good way to explore timbre because of the many types of instruments –*
   - See if you have CD collections of musical pieces played by different musical instruments in your own music library. Then, categorize the music in terms of musical instruments being played. For example:
   - <u>Percussion</u> such as Conga[1]
   - <u>Woodwind</u> such as Flute[2] or Saxophone[3] *Coltrane – saxophone Kenny G*
   - <u>String</u> such as Violin[4]
   - <u>Keyboard</u> such as Piano[5] *John Maher, Nora Jones*
   - What I Have:

   - Research other music collections where can you can find the same music played by different musical instruments. For example:
   - "Ave Maria" played by Cello & Voice[6] vs. Harp & Voice[7]
   - My search:

   { Bach – Four Suites for Orchestra Arranged for <u>Guitar</u>
   – Brazilian Guitar Quartet
   The Amsterdam <u>Baroque</u> Orchestra – Four Bach Suites
   The Four <u>Lute</u> Suites – John Williams.

   Bach – Four Suites

---

[1] "Patato" played by Legendary Cuban conga master in The Big Bang (1997). *The Big Bang: An Explosive Exploration of Percussion Music from Around the Planet.* NY: Ellipsis Arts

[2] *The Instruments of Classical Music Vol.1: The Flute.* Los Angeles, CA: Delta Music Inc.

[3] Kenny G. (1994). *Miracles: The Holiday Album.* New York:ARISTA.

[4] ADRM (Digital Remaster to Audiophile Standards). (1988). Mozart for Morning Coffee. New York: London Records

[5] George Winston. (1982). *December:* George Winston Piano Solo. Indiana: Windham Hill Records.

[6] Yo-Yo Ma & Bobby McFerrin. (1992). Yo-Yo Ma Bobby McFerrin Hush. New York: Sony Music Entertainment Inc.

[7] Kathleen Battle. (1997). Grace. New York: Sony Music Entertainment Inc.

2. Talk about timbre-effect in music.
   - Discuss how the image of music is influenced by which musical instruments are being played[1]
   - The image I drew in mind when listened to the musical piece:
     Horses galloping free
   - What kind of musical instruments were used to represent a certain character? For example:
   - In *Peter and the wolf*[2], a bird was played by a flute, a duck by oboe, a cat by clarinet, a grandfather by bassoon, a wolf by French horn, a boy by stringed orchestra, and guns of the hunter by drum.

3. Discuss what kinds of activities you can do with children to feel timbre.
   - Children can express what they hear. For example,
   - Word expression: Describe the sound with adjectives.
   - Draw the image of a musical story
   - My idea: Draw an abstract picture of lines + colors that describe the timbre
   - Children can replace the sounds with other instrumental sounds they can play. For example,
   - In the music *Peter and the wolf*, each character can be played by a percussion instrument children can play.
   - My idea: Use different body sounds + voice
   - Children can make musical sounds for the story they know. For example:
   - In the story Three Little Pigs, when each pig builds the house, the sound can be different (e.g., brick house played by tic-tock block, straw house by guiro, etc.)
   - My idea: The Little Red Hen → use instruments for animals when they say "No!"
   - Children can create their own musical story, so they can use their own musical idea.

---

[1] "Old Castle" played by different musical instruments from the video tape Music Appreciation: Music… is Tone Color. CA: Valencia Entertainment.
[2] Boston Pops Orchestra (1988). *Classics for Children*. New York: BMG Music.

Reflection on Unit 1

1. At this juncture, what is your personal definition of:
   - Sounds
   - Timbre

2. What musical activities will you use in the classroom to:
   - Explore sounds of environment and nature
   - Make sounds of body and voice
   - Create sounds using objects and musical instruments

3. My reflection on the musical experience in Unit 1.
   - With respect to my personal learning and growth
   - In terms of my future teaching experience

Sound is a noise, vocal sound or musical tone that is audible. Timbre is the quality of sound that evokes an image or distinguishes one instrument from another.

Listening walks are good ways to explore sound. They can be accompanied by a worksheet to record sounds or pencils + paper to draw. CD's or tapes of sounds can be played for the children to guess at what the sound is such as ocean or bell etc.

To explore body sounds or voice the children can experiment and share ways to make sounds. They can play separately + try to mimic each other and/or play as a band. Children when introduced to instruments can try and guess how to play them before you show them. They can come up with different ways to play them. Children can be asked to try + replicate a rhythm or create a rhythm. children can use the ~~different~~ instruments to represent characters in a story that they know or make up together.

I enjoyed making a group song using only body sounds because it showed me how you can

Each instrument is special because it makes its own unique sound.

connect with others + create something.

It would be a good exercise to use in the classroom. The idea of using instruments to represent characters ~~can~~ such as in the Peter and the Wolf but in a simplified manner would definitely be something that I know the children would enjoy and I will try out in the classroom.

Unit 2: Beat, Rhythm, and Meter

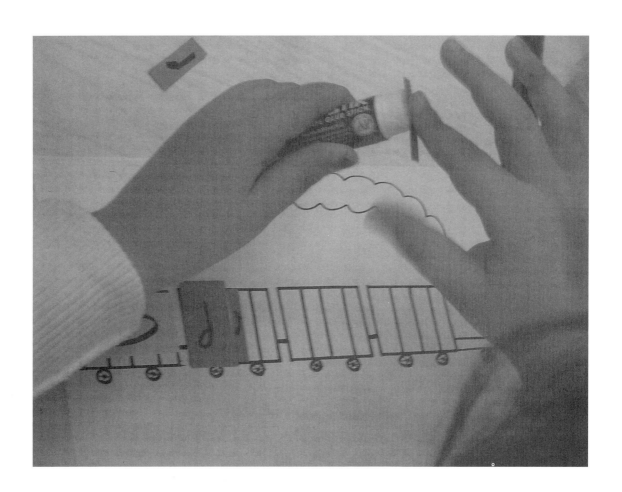

Beat
*

Metrical pulse

.

A steady pulse that you can clap
throughout music

Meter
*

Basic grouping of beats
such as two, three, four, or six beats.

Rhythm
*

The pattern of movement in time

.

It is patterns of
long and short sounds in a group

Unit 2
Beat, Rhythm, and Meter

You will learn and reflect on music and teaching through:

2-1. Building Knowledge

2-1-(1) Beat and Meter
2-1-(2) Rhythm and Beat

2-2. Developing Skills

2-2-(1) Acting Rhythm
2-2-(2) Visual Rhythm
2-2-(3) Symbolic Rhythm

2-3. Experiencing

2-3-(1) Cultural Rhythm and Beat
2-3-(2) Rhythm and Beat in Music

2-1. Building Knowledge
2-1-(1) Beat and Meter

Activity 2-1-(1)

1. Do the following activity to learn the concept of a Beat.
   - <u>2 Beats</u>
   - Bring 2 different colors of materials such as buttons or candies (You need at least 2 buttons for each color)
   - Make a pattern so that you can have a repetition of two different colors of buttons (e.g., Red-Yellow, Red-Yellow...)

One Two |One Two

   - Clap your hands for each button, counting "one-two-one-two."
   - Now, give a strong clap for the first button in a group, still counting "one" and "'two." (Each clap should be steady in terms of timing.)
   - Think of what kind of music can fit for this beat (e.g., March).
   - Clap for the beat while listening to music in 2 beats.

   - <u>3 Beats</u>
   - Rearrange the button so that you can have 3 buttons in a group
      (e.g., Red- Yellow-Yellow, Red-Yellow-Yellow...).

One Two Three | One Two Three

   - Clap for each button, counting '"One-two-three-one-two-three."
   - Give a strong clap for the first button of a group (Each clap should be steady in timing.)
   - Think of what kind of music would fit for this beat (e.g., waltz).
   - Clap the beat, listening to the music in 3 beats

   - <u>4 Beats</u>
   - Rearrange the button so that you can have 4 buttons in a group
      (e.g., Red-Yellow-Blue-Yellow, Red-Yellow-Blue-Yellow...)

One Two Three Four |One Two Three Four

- Clap for each button, counting one-two-three-four.
- Give a strong clap for the first button, medium strong clap for the third button, and soft clap for rest of the buttons in a group. (Each clap should be steady in timing.)
- Think of what kind of music would fit for this beat (Most children's songs would fit 4 beats.)
- Clap for the beat while listening or singing to the music in 4 beats.

2. Define Beat and Meter in your own words.
    - Research the definition of those terms in dictionaries.
    - *Meter* is the pattern in which a steady succession of rhythmic pulses is organized.[1]
    - *Beat* is a metrical pulse. It is also the marking of such a pulse by movements of the hand in conducting.[2]
    - My search: *Meter — the rhythmic element as measured by div. into parts of equal time value.*
      Beat — to mark time by stroke as with hand or metronome

      meter.
      The unit of meas. in terms of # of beats, adopted for a given piece of music.

    - Make the definition easy so that the children can understand. For example:
    - *Beat* is a steady pulse as you clap throughout a musical piece.
    - *Meter* is the basic grouping of beats such as two, three, four, or six beats.
    - My definition: *Measurement in terms of number of beats*

3. Share some ideas of some other ways of making a rhythmic pattern.
    - What kind of visual materials or pictures can we use to make a pattern?
    - Pictures with themes such as animals.
    - Season or Holiday-related picture pattern
    - My idea: *Different shape blocks*
      Shape patterns

    - What are other ways of making sound to match visual patterns?
    - Clapping
    - Tapping
    - My idea: *Snapping*

    - Think of the physical environment in a classroom setting where children might find patterns. For example:
    - Manipulative materials
    - Wallpaper
    - My finding: *Rug - colored squares*

---

[1] Randel, D. M. (ed.). (1986). *The New Harvard Dictionary of Music*. MA: The Belknap Press of Harvard University Press

[2] Randel, D. M. (ed.). (1986). *The New Harvard Dictionary of Music*. MA: The Belknap Press of Harvard University Press

2-1. Building Knowledge
2-1-(2) Rhythm and Beat

Activity 2-1-(2)

---

1. Do the following activity to learn the concepts of Rhythm and Beat.
   - Rhythm in a Beat
   - Make a pattern for 2 beats such as "Red-Yellow, Red-Yellow…"
   - Stomp your feet for each button, in a steady beat.
   - While stomping, call out the color of each button, "Red, Yel-low…"
   - Clap hands to match each syllable. In other words, you clap once for red and twice for yellow. (When you clap twice, you should divide the time evenly for each clap.)
   - Stomp your feet to match each button (beat) and clap for syllables (rhythm).

With eyes	●	●	●	●	
Counting in mind	1	2	1	2	Beat
With Feet	Stomp	Stomp	Stomp	Stomp	
With voice	Red	Yel-low	Red	Yel-low	Rhythm
With hands	Clap	Clap-clap	Clap	Clap-clap	

   - Arrange the buttons in 3 and 4 beats and do the same activity.

   - Rhythmic Pattern
   - Everybody stomps feet in steady 2 beats.
   - One person makes one rhythmic pattern and keeps clapping while others keep stomping.
   - Other people repeat after the person.
   - The next person makes another pattern and claps while others keep stomping,
   - My pattern (Write or draw your pattern in any form so that you can recognize when and how to play):

2. Define Rhythm
    - Research definition from a dictionary.
      - *Rhythm* is a pattern of movement in time[1]
      - *My search:* Movement or procedure with uniform or patterned recurrence of a beat, accent or the like
    - Define the term in your own words.
      - *Rhythm* is patterns of long and short sounds in a group.
      - *My definition:* Rhythm is a pattern of sounds of different lengths

3. Think of other ways to learn the concept of rhythm.
    - You can watch good videotapes to teach the concept. For example:
      - Why Toes Tap[2]

    - You can use children's rhymes or poems for rhythm. For instance:
      - Read children's poems rhythmically
      - Make different rhythms for the same word
      - Clap along with rhythms
      - My idea: Use syllables in childrens names
        Use dance steps or body movements w a rhythmical pattern

---

[1] Randel, D. M. (ed.). (1986). *The New Harvard Dictionary of Music.* MA: The Belknap Press of Harvard University Press

[2] Marsalis, J. (1995). *Marsalis on Music*: '*Why Toes Tap*' with Seiji Ozawa. VHS. NY: Sony Music Entertainment Inc.

2-2. Developing Skills
2-2-(1) Acting Rhythm

Activity 2-2-(1)

1. The following activity is to help you understand concepts of musical terms, beat, rhythm, and meter.
    - Read the following sign to represent 4 beats in a measure.

    - The picture represents the capacity of a room.
    - The sign above means that you have a room for 4 numbers of adults

    - Prepare 4 seats to represent for 4 beats in a measure. For example:

    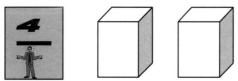

    - The chairs are for 4 adults to sit on.
    - You cannot take out any chair even when nobody sits on a chair because the sign says you need a room for 4 adults.

    - Find a way to make sound for each beat. The following is an example.

    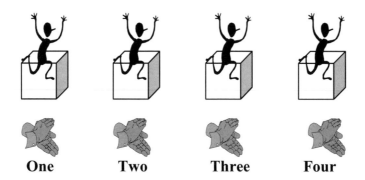

One	Two	Three	Four

    - Let 4 people come and sit in each chair.
    - Clap for each person, counting one-two-three-four.
    - Your counting should be steady in timing.

- Find a way to keep the beat even when you do not make sound.

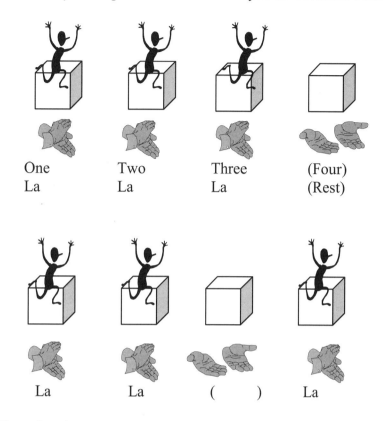

- Even though you have three people, you still have four seats (beats).
- Counting one through four in a steady beat, clap for the people sitting on chairs and take a rest (not clapping) for the empty seat.
- Rearrange the people so that you can have a different spot of an empty seat and clap for each person on the seat.
- Use your voice and say "La" for each person on a seat, instead of clapping.

- Find a way to hold the sound for two beats.

- Let's say that there is a big man who takes two seats.
- Say "La" for each person as you did. However, for the chairs a big person sits on, you need to hold "La ~" for two seats (=beats).
- Tell how it is different from previous ones where you had one empty seat.
- Try other combinations such as the person taking the first and second seats (La ~, La, La)

- Find a way you can make two sounds in a beat.

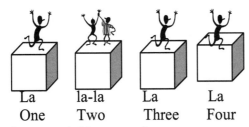

- Let's say that two children can share one seat.
- You should still count one, two, three, and four in your mind in a steady beat.
  But, you say "la-la" in a seat where two children share the seat.
- Try other combinations such as children sharing the third chair (La, La, la-la, La).

2. Create activities you might do with children using acting symbols.
   - Find a simple rhythmic pattern of a poem or a song and make acting symbols to match a rhythmic pattern of the poem. For example:
   - Twinkle

   - Beginning part of "Carol of the bells"

   - How can you use acting symbols in your class? For example:
   - A game: Make rhythmic sounds according to acting symbols or vice versa
   - My idea:

2-2. Developing Skills
2-2-(2) Visual Rhythm

Activity 2-2-(2)

---

1. You can learn the same concept using visual symbols or math manipulatives.
   - Musical concepts can be explained using mathematical concepts. The following is an example to represent 4 beats in a measure.

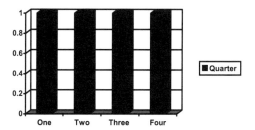

   - How many black bars are there? (four)
   - How tall is each bar? (1: See the number on the left side)
   - What is the total number of four bars? (1+1+1+1=4)
   - Clap for each bar, counting one, two, three, and four in a steady beat.
   - Repeat it several times, until you get used to clap in a steady beat.

   - Each beat can be broken down.

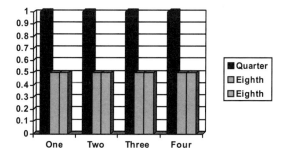

   - How many bars do we need if we break each black bar into two pieces? (8)
   - How tall is each gray bar? (1/2 or 0.5)
   - Count one, two, three, and four as we did in the previous activity.
   - Clap twice in each count. Each clap should be even in each count.
   - How many times do we clap in four counts?

- Make different combinations using black and gray bars. For example:

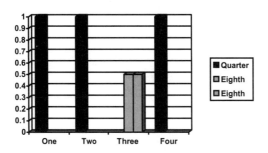

- Clap matching each bar, counting one, two, three, and four in a steady beat.
- You should clap twice evenly in the third beat.
- The pattern above matches B-I-NG-O part of "Bingo" song. Sing the song while clapping.

2. Share ideas on how we can help children learn the concept of rhythm using visual material.
    - To represent a group of beats, you can use different visual aids. For example:
    - A car of a train
    - My idea:
    Pictures of buildings
    - Rhythmic patterns can be represented by different visual materials. For example:
    - One dog for one beat and two puppies for two half beats.
    - An apple for one beat and two half pieces of apples for two half beats.
    - My idea:
    One pizza — slices of pizza in diff sizes
    $\frac{1}{2}, \frac{1}{4}, \frac{1}{8}$

2-2. Developing Skills
2-2-(3) Symbolic Rhythm

1. Learn about Meter and Measure.

Measure Bar
Meter Signature (or Time Signature)

[Figure 2-2-(3)] Meter and Measure

- Research and learn about meter signature. For example:
- *Meter* is like timing of music.
- Meter is represented by meter signature
- The number on the top directs how many beats are played in a group
- Here, 4 on the top means that you play 4 beats in a group. If you see 3 on the top, that means you play 3 beats in a group
- The number 4 in the bottom decides which note symbol will be counted as one beat.
- Here, 4 stands for a quarter-note beat, meaning that quarter note will last for one beat. (Note symbols will be explained in the following activity.)

- Research and learn about measure. For example:
- A *Measure* is a visual representation of meter.
- Each measure provides the notation for a rhythmic pattern in a group.
- A measure is separated by a vertical line called a *Measure bar*. In other words, measure bar is a divider to put notes in a group.

2. Learn about different note and rest values.
   - Research and learn the name of each musical note and rest symbols and how long each symbol lasts or rests. For example[1]:

[Table 2-2-(3)] Musical symbols

Symbol		Name	Value	
Note	Rest	Note or Rest	Lasts for	Rests for
𝅝	▬	Whole	4 beats	
𝅗𝅥	▬	Half	2 beats	
𝅘𝅥	𝄽	Quarter	1 beat	
𝅘𝅥𝅮	𝄾	Eighth	1/2 beat	
𝅘𝅥𝅯	𝄿	Sixteenth	1/4 beat	

Dotted Notes / Dotted Rests	The same as…	Extend to Last or Rest for	Total Duration
𝅝.	dotted whole note	4 + 2	6 beats
▬.	dotted whole note rest		
𝅗𝅥.	dotted half note	2+1	3 beats
▬.	dotted half note rest		
𝅘𝅥.	dotted quarter note	1+1/2	1 ½ beat
𝄽.	dotted quarter note rest		
𝅘𝅥𝅮.	dotted eighth note	1/2 + 1/4	3/4 beat
𝄾.	dotted eighth note rest		

---

[1] http://library.thinkquest.org/15413/theory/note-reading.htm#values

- See if you understood the concept by explaining it. For example:
- A dot to the right of a note extends its duration by 50 percent.
- A half note lasts for 2 beats and a dotted half note lasts for 3 (2+1) beats. In other words, a dot next to a half note extends the duration by 50% (1 beat) of half note (2 beats).
- In playing, a dotted half note is different from a half note and a quarter note. You play a half note holding 2 beats and play a quarter note holding one beat. However, once you play the dotted half note you hold it for 3 beats.

3. Think about how you can integrate the concept for children.
   - Create an activity children can do to experience the concept of different notes or rests. For example:
   - Clap along with different notes. Divide into 5 groups and each group takes a role for each note. For instance, the group for a whole note claps every 4 beats while the group for a half note claps every 2 beats.
   - You can also arrange the notes and rests and clap or rest along with those symbols.
   - My idea:

   - Using the symbols above, make a game you can do with the children you are teaching. For example:
   - Counting game: Count numbers in a steady beat. When you see a quarter note symbol, you call the number. However, when you see a rest note symbol you should not call out (but just count in your mind).
   - My idea:

2-3. Experiencing
2-3-(1) Cultural Rhythm and Beat

Activity 2-3-(1)

1. Research rhythm & beat from different cultures.
   - If you have an electronic keyboard, you can play some basic rhythm and beat just by selecting numbers.

   - You can use recorded music: The following[1] are some examples.
   - Legendary Cuban Conga master "Patato"
   - Six Man Ugandan Xylophone by "Amampondo"
   - "Glen Velez" on Egyptian tambourine
   - My search: Drummers of Burundi

2. Listen to the musical pieces with traditional rhythms from other cultures and countries.
   - What do you feel when you hear the music? What is your impression?

   - What are the sounds from the musical instruments you hear?

   - What is the rhythm and beat you hear?
   - Move to the beat and rhythm
   - Copy the beat with percussion instruments.

3. Share your ideas about how you can help children explore and feel cultural rhythm and beat.
   - Can you find any part of the music children can play along with?

   - How can the beat or rhythm be presented using figures or musical symbols?

---

[1] The Big Bang (1997) *The Big Bang: An Explosive Exploration of Percussion Music From Around the Planet.* NY: Ellipsis Arts

2-3. Experiencing
2-3-(2) Rhythmic and Beat in Music

Activity 2-3-(2)

1. You can feel rhythm and beat while playing music.
    - Make a group for a rhythmic band.
      - Have members of 4 or 5 people in a group.
      - Each member gets one or two percussion instruments

    - Create rhythmic music in your band.
      - Make a simple rhythmic pattern for each instrument.
      - Arrange rhythmic patterns of each instrument and write down what and how your group plays.
      - The patterns can be repeated, played one after another, or at the same time.

    - Each group performs a rhythmic piece.
      - Record the music of the group's performance

2. You can share your feeling and thoughts.
    - What did you feel? When you:
      - Create the pattern
      - Practice with your group
      - Perform for the class
      - Listen to other groups' performances
      - Listen to your group's performance on the recorded tape.
      - Etc.

    - What were the differences? When you:
      - Plan and play
      - Play and listen to other groups' performances
      - Play in your group and listen to your group's performance on the tape

3. You can help children feel rhythm and beat while playing.
    - What kind of activities can you do with children? For example:
      - Marching band: children can make and play rhythmic patterns for each instrument.
      - My idea: chant a rhyme while playing an instrument in the rhythm of the words.

Reflection on Unit 2

1. At this juncture, what is your personal definition of:
   - Beat
   - Meter
   - Measure
   - Rhythm

2. What musical activities will you use in the classroom to:
   - Learn rhythmic concepts by acting
   - Learn the concept of musical rhythm using visual materials.
   - Learn musical note and rest symbols

3. My reflection on the musical experience in Unit 2.
   - With respect to my personal learning and growth
   - In terms of my future teaching experience

Beat is the pulse that is constant throughout the piece

Meter is the grouping of notes ~~continuous this beat~~ that ~~give the~~ is the time signature

Measure is the

Rhythm is the pattern of notes.

The activity with the chairs + clapping for the number of people on the chairs is an excellent activity for the Pre-K class. It was an interesting description of a room where only 4 chairs are allowed or ~~three~~ chairs ee but the # of people sitting on them can vary. This is something that the children know and can connect with. You can connect this to a story such as "The Three Little Pigs." The buttons that show how to clap rhythms to the children is a very simple and effective way to translate rhythm to visual symbols.

To help children learn the music notes it would be a good idea to make them into characters such as Mr Half note or Little Miss Quarter note because the younger children relate to ~~these~~ characters as well as symbols. It would be fun to have the

> *Beat gives me stability, while rhythm gives me fun when it gives a variation within and around a beat.*

children help name them.

I have used instruments and music a lot in the classroom but ~~these~~ ideas will help me make the concepts more relatable to a younger group + will give them a more in depth knowledge.

Unit 3: Tempo and Dynamics

Tempo
*

Slowness and fastness of music

It is the speed
at which music is performed

Dynamics
*

The aspect of music
relating to
the degree of loudness and quietness

Unit 3
Tempo and Dynamics

You will learn and reflect on music and teaching through:

3-1. Building Knowledge

3-1-(1) Tempo
3-1-(2) Dynamics

3-2. Developing Skills

3-2-(1) Listening Activities
3-2-(2) Activities with Symbols

3-3. Experiencing

3-3-(1) Feeling in Music
3-3-(2) Tempo and Dynamics in Music

3-1. Building Knowledge
3-1-(1) Tempo

Activity 3-1-(1)

1. Define Tempo
   - Find the term in a music dictionary.
   - A speed at which music is performed.[1]
   - The rate per unit of time of metrical pulses in performances.[2]
   - My search: *Relative rapidity or rate of movement usually indicated by such terms as "adagio, allegro etc. or by reference to the metronome.*
   - Make the definition using easy words so that the children can understand. For example:
   - Fastness or slowness of music playing
   - My definition: *The tempo is how fast or slow the music plays.*

2. Explore tempo to learn the concept.
   - You can use a metronome.
   - Listening to the tempo made in a metronome by sounding regular beats at adjustable speed.
   - Watching the movement of the needle or blinking light (with an electric metronome) in different tempo.
   - Moving your hands or singing along to the beat.

   - You can use an electric keyboard.
   - Using the function to change the tempo.
   - Listening to the same rhythm in different tempo.

---

[1] Randel, D. M. (ed.). (1986). *The New Harvard Dictionary of Music*. MA: The Belknap Press of Harvard University Press

[2] Randel, D. M. (ed.). (1986). *The New Harvard Dictionary of Music*. MA: The Belknap Press of Harvard University Press

3-1. Building Knowledge
3-1-(2) Dynamics

Activity 3-1-(2)

1. Define the term Dynamics.
    - Find the term in a music dictionary.
    - The aspect of music relating to degrees of loudness[1]
    - My search: variation and gradation in the volume of musical sound.
    - Make the definition using easy words so that the children can understand. For example:
    - Loudness or quietness of music.
    - My definition: The way that the music gets louder or quieter as it is played.

2. Explore the concept Dynamics
    - Play a percussion instrument such as a drum at different degrees of loudness.
    - Loud/Quiet
    - Very loud/Very quiet
    - Medium loud/Medium quiet
    - Gradually louder/Gradually quieter

    - Dynamics must be combined with tempo. However, a certain degree of loudness doesn't necessarily mean to be played in a certain tempo. Play a drum in different combination of tempo and dynamics. For example:
    - Loud and fast
    - Loud and slow
    - Quiet and fast
    - Quiet and slow

---

[1] Randel, D. M. (ed.). (1986). *The New Harvard Dictionary of Music*. MA: The Belknap Press of Harvard University Press

3-2. Developing Skills
3-2-(1) Listening Activities

Activity 3-2-(1)

1. Listen to musical pieces in different tempos and dynamics.
   - Search for musical pieces played in different tempo and dynamics. For example:
   - In *Saint-Saeng's Carnival of Animals*, "The Swan" (Quiet and Slow), "The Elephant" (Loud and Slow), and so forth.
   - My listening: *The Nutcracker Suite*

2. Describe different tempos and dynamics of the music you listened to.
   - You can describe the mood of music in words. For example:
   - Listening to fast music: Busy, rush, chase, etc.
   - Listening to slow music: Soothing, relaxed, calm, etc.
   - Listening to loud music: Heavy, noisy, etc.
   - Listening to quiet music: Quiet, hiding, peaceful, etc.

   - Reflecting tempo and dynamics of music, you can draw how you feel listening to the music.
   - Using lines, dots, or other shapes.
   - Using different colors.
   - Draw a picture of your imagination.

3. Brainstorm when you can use music in different tempo and dynamics in your class.
   - Background music
   - Rest or nap time (slow and quiet)
   - Clean-up time (fast and not too loud)
   - Outdoor play (moderately fast and loud)

   - With other activities
   - Art: Finger painting listening to the music in different tempos and dynamics
   - Movement: Walk or run in different tempo and dynamics
   - My idea: Action rhymes such as row the boat or head, shoulders, knees + toes can be performed at different tempos + dynamics together

3-2. Developing Skills
3-2-(2) Activities with Symbols

Activity 3-2-(2)

1. Learn about special symbols to present Dynamics.
    *   Memorize the name and meaning of the symbols in the following table.

Symbols	Read as	Meaning
pp	pianissimo	Very quiet
P	piano	Quiet
mp	mezzo piano	Moderately quiet
mf	mezzo forte	Moderately loud
f	forte	Loud
ff	fortissimo	Very loud
<	crescendo	Gradually louder
> *decresc.* *dim.*	decrescendo diminuendo	Gradually quieter

>	Accent	Stress the note

2. Using the symbols, create an activity or a game you can do with children in class.
    *   Make visual materials to show different symbols you might be using for children.
    -   Flash cards for each symbol
    -   Symbol sticks to hold and pick up to respond to dynamics.
    -   Stickers to be attached on words or musical notes of a song.

    *   You can use the symbol to direct how to sing or play.
    -   Sing/play loud when a conductor picks *forte'* sign
    -   Sing/play quiet when a conductor picks *piano* sign
    -   Sing/play gradually louder when a conductor picks *crescendo* sign

    *   Children can use the symbol.
    -   Listening to musical pieces, children can pick up the cards to respond to dynamics.
    -   My idea:

3-3. Experiencing
3-3-(1) Feeling in Music

Activity 3-3-(1)

1. Listen to the music in different tempo and dynamics.
   - Usually *Sonata* has different parts. For example:
   - Beethoven, Sonata No. 8 "Pathetique"; Grave-Allegro & Adagio Cantabile
   - Beethoven, Sonata No. 14 "Moonlight"; Adagio sostenuto & Presto Agitato

   - You can go to a concert of rhythmic band or watch the video tape to observe and listen to a performance of a professional rhythmic band. For example:
   - Stomp Outloud[1]

2. Share your feeling.
   - How did you feel listening to different parts of Sonata?

   - How did the music (player) make a different tempo or dynamics? In *Stomp outloud* for example:
   - By playing different instruments such as pots and pans.
   - By adding more instruments
   - Your example:

   By using body movements to portray a rest eg. swinging

---

[1] Stomp Outloud. VHS. 1997. New York: Yes/No Productions Ltd.

3-3. Experiencing
3-3-(2) Tempo and Dynamics in Music

Activity 3-3-(2)

1. Do the following activity to explore dynamics.
    *   Example: Raindance
    -   Sit in a big circle
    -   You will play 5 different sounds: 1) Finger snapping, 2) Rubbing hands, 3) Rolling fingers on the table, 4) Tapping Thighs, and 5) Stomping Feet.
    -   The conductor goes around the circle directing what sound you will play. Until s/he re-directs you to the next sound, keep playing the sound.
    -   The conductor begins with 1) finger snapping sound and goes around with the next sound 2).
    -   When all people are stomping feet, the conductor goes around again. This time, go backwards of 4), 3), 2), and 1). When every body is snapping their fingers, the conductor, going around one more time slowly, will let them stop the sound.
    -   If you record it and play it back, you will hear a rainy sound.

2. Create rhythmic music in a group.
    *   Make a music band from the group.
    -   Have members of 4 or 5 people.
    -   Each member can have a percussion instrument, use body percussion, or a voice.
    -   Make a simple rhythmic pattern for each instrument. (You can use the same music you created in the previous unit.)
    -   Add dynamics and tempo.
    -   Record your rhythmic pattern using dynamic symbols as well as different shapes, lines, or so forth.

    *   Practice several times and perform.
    -   Each group performs a rhythmic piece.
    -   Record each group's performance.
    -   When every group is finished, listen to the recordings.

    *   Share your feeling. For example:
    -   How did you feel planning, practicing, playing, and listening?
    -   What was your most favorite (or difficult) part? And why?

Reflection on Unit 3

1. At this juncture, what is your personal definition of:
   - Tempo
   - Dynamics

2. What musical activities will you use in the classroom to:
   - Listen and respond to the music in different tempos and dynamics
   - Play music in different tempos and dynamics

3. My reflection on the musical experience in Unit 3.
   - With respect to my personal learning and growth
   - In terms of my future teaching experience

I will use the activity where the children draw their expressions to the music. I will have them move in different ways to express the tempo and feeling of the music. Having the children sing slow or fast and loud or soft is a fun activity. Sometimes we do "Head Shoulders, Knees, Toes" or "Row the Boat" at different tempos.

I enjoyed the video which showed how changing the meter of the music completely changed the feel and of the music from the Nutcracker Suite. The presenter used everyday examples to teach the children about musical terms such as bars, rhythm, melody etc. which the children could relate to such as basketball, traffic flow, food etc. This relationship between things the children know and things they need to learn is a technique that i can use in the classroom. In Stomp I enjoyed the way that everyday objects could be used + played

Depending on how we play it, music can be fast or slow, loud or quiet.

in different ways to produce different dynamics. The children could find an object in the classroom + try to play a in different ways. Music can be made with a low budget in interesting ways.

Unit 4: Pitch, Melody, and Harmony

Pitch
*

Highness and lowness of sound

.

A sound can be high, low, or in between.

Melody
*

Coherent succession of pitch and rhythm

.

A pitch with rhythm can flow...
up, down, or repeat the same

Harmony
*

Simultaneous sounding of two or more pitches

.

Two or more different pitches can be
sounded at the same time

Unit 4
Pitch, Melody, and Harmony

You will learn and reflect on music and teaching through:

4-1. Building Knowledge

4-1-(1) Pitch
4-1-(2) Melody
4-1-(3) Harmony

4-2. Developing Skills

4-2-(1) Pitch-Learning Activities
4-2-(2) Melodic Activities
4-2-(3) Harmonic Activities

4-3. Experiencing

4-3-(1) Pitch and Melody in Music
4-3-(2) Melody and Harmony in Music

4-1. Building Knowledge
4-1-(1) Pitch

Activity 4-1-(1)

1. Explore the Pitch.
    - Brainstorm where we can find highness or lowness of sound and try to imitate the sound. For example:
      - *Female voices usually make high sounds while male voices make low sounds.*
      - *Birds chirp high while lions growl low*
      - *A siren repeats high and low sounds*

    - Explore an object with which you can make high and/or low sound. For example:
      - *Rubber band when stretched or loosened*
      - *Glasses filled with water in different height*
      - *Pieces of metal in different sizes*
      - *My idea:* Bamboo of different lengths

    - Explore the sound of pitched musical instruments that make a stable and clear pitch. For example:
      - *Stringed instruments: guitar, etc.*
      - *Keyboard instruments: piano, etc.*
      - *Pitched percussion instruments: xylophone, etc.*
      - *Wind instruments: recorder, etc.*

2. Discuss ways to make/play different pitches in the classroom.
    - Discuss how you can make a high or low sound with objects.
      - *The tighter the string is, the higher the pitch sounds; the thinner the string is, the higher the pitch sounds (rubber band and stringed instrument)*
      - *The shorter the bar is, the higher the pitch sounds (xylophone)*
      - *The shorter the height is, the higher the pitch sounds (glass of water)*

    - Discuss how you can make different pitch in playing musical instruments.
      - *When you bang on the shorter bars on a xylophone, you make a higher sound.*
      - *On keyboard instruments such as the piano, when you play left to right, you can make a low to high sound.*
      - *Plucking thinner string, you can make higher pitch.*
      - *Plucking the same line in a string instrument such as the guitar, you can make a higher pitch when you press frets (a strip of material placed across the fingerboard or neck of a stringed instrument).*

3. Define Pitch.
- Research how pitch is defined in music dictionaries.
    - Pitch is the perceived quality of a sound that is chiefly a function of its fundamental frequency.[1]
    - A stretch of sound whose frequency is clear and stable enough to be heard as not noise.[2]
    - My search: Determine the key or keynote of the particular tonal standard with which given tones are compared in respect to their relative level
- Define pitch in your own words. For example:
    - A High and low sound that is clear and stable enough to be heard.
    - My definition:

    How high or low a sound is heard

---

[1] Randel, D. M. (1986). *The New Harvard Dictionary of Music*. MA: The Belknap Press of Harvard University Press.
[2] Randel, D. M. (1986). *The New Harvard Dictionary of Music*. MA: The Belknap Press of Harvard University Press.

4-1. Building Knowledge
4-1-(2) Melody

Activity 4-1-(2)

1. Define Melody.
   - Search the definition of melody in a music dictionary. For example:
   - Melody is a coherent succession of pitches[1]
   - My search: *musical sounds in agreeable succession or arrangement*
   - Define the term in your own words. For example:
   - Melody is moving pitch partnered with rhythm
   - My definition: *the flow of different pitches which form a rhythmic sound*

2. Explore Melody.
   - Brainstorm where you can hear a melody. For example:
   - Music box
   - Cellular phone signal
   - Ice cream truck
   - Songs
   - My finding: *Radio, films & T.V. elevator*

   - Discuss how melody is made out of pitch. For example:
   - While pitch refers to a sound of a certain highness, melody is a flow of sound that flows up, down, or repeats.
   - Pitch is partnered with rhythm to be melody. In other words, melody has rhythm in it, holding a sound for certain beats and resting.

---

[1] Randel, D. M. (1986). *The New Harvard Dictionary of Music*. MA: The Belknap Press of Harvard University Press.

4-1. Building Concepts
4-1-(3) Harmony

Activity 4-1-(3)

1. Define Harmony in your own words.
   - Search for the term in a music dictionary
   - The relationship of tones considered as they sound simultaneously, and the way such relationships are organized in time[1]
   - Any particular collection of pitches sounded simultaneously, termed a chord.
   - My search:
     any simultaneous combination of tones
   - Paraphrase with easy-to-understand words.
   - Two or more pitches sounded together
   - My definition:
     Pitches played together that are pleasant to hear

2. Brainstorm where you can hear the sound of harmony.
   For example:
   - With voice
   - Duet songs
   - Choir
   - Accapella where voices harmonize without musical instrument accompaniment

   - With musical instruments
   - Piano Duet (Duo) where two people play a song on a piano
   - Trio such as violin, cello, and piano playing together
   - Orchestra music

3. Explore a harmonic sound.
   - Discuss the conditions or ways to make a harmonic sound.
   - You need at least 2 different notes
   - Played at the same time.
   - My idea:
     Sing two songs such as Mary Had a Little Lamb + Twinkle Twinkle Little Star together
   - Explore musical instruments with which you can make harmony. For example:
   - Pressing a chord button of autoharp and strum strings.
   - Selecting chord for harmonic accompaniment with an electric keyboard.
   - My thought:
     Use chime bars played together

---

[1] Randel, D. M. (1986). *The New Harvard Dictionary of Music*. MA: The Belknap Press of Harvard University Press.

4-2. Developing Skills
4-2-(1) Pitch-Learning Activities

Activity 4-2-(1)

1. Learn the basic concepts of symbols to present different pitch.
    *   Search the names of basic symbols to draw musical notes in different pitch and define each word. For example:

    -   <u>Staff</u>: five lines (=four spaces) to draw music on

    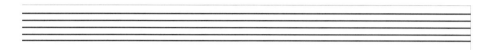

    -   <u>G (treble) clef</u>: a symbol to indicate special positions of pitches

    -   <u>Scale</u>: Underlying set of tones for melody (e.g., C scale)

    -   <u>Ledger lines</u>: short lines to draw the notes beyond (lower or higher than) 5 lines of staff.

    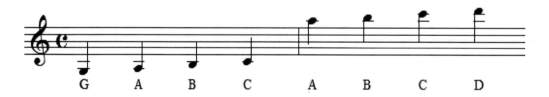

- Find rules in drawing symbols. For example:
- Notes can be drawn on lines.

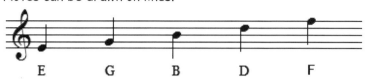

- Notes can be drawn in spaces.

- On a staff the higher the note is, the higher the pitch sounds.

- Play each note on a xylophone or any other keyboard instrument. For example:
- You can match each pitch with an alphabet letter on the board of a xylophone.
- You will see the same set of alphabets such as C and C on your xylophone. One is long and the other is short. In other words, one is low and the other is high.
- You can compare the sound of different pitches.

2. Discuss ways to teach the pitch concept
   - You can find ways to teach symbols. For example:
   - Making up a story: There was a family, a father (Adam), a mother (Betty), and five sons (Ceasar), (David), (Eddy), (Frank), and (George). They lived in a building with 5 lines and 4 spaces.
   - My idea: There was a group of ants that lived in an anthill with 5 rooms + 4 tunnels between
   - You can create a game or a musical activity on pitch. For example:
   - Imitate sounds of different pitch a teacher plays
   - Make a high or low sound when a conductor points high or low position.
   - Listening to high or low pitch played on a xylophone, move body (or hands) up or down, or vice versa.
   - Answer a question with high pitch for "yes" and low pitch for "no" and so forth.
   - My idea:

4-2. Developing Skills
4-2-(2) Melodic Activities

Activity 4-2-(2)

1. Read and play a Melody
   - Read melodies of children's songs. For example:

   - - Find each note on a xylophone
   - - Describe how a pitch moves (up, down, or repeat)
   - - Read it along with the rhythm
   - - You can make your own reading table. For example:

Beat	1	2	3	4	1	2	3	(4)	1	2	3	4
Pitch	C	C	G	G	A	A	G	-	F	F	E	E

   - Play it with a rhythm.
   - - You can count one-two-three-four for four beats.
   - - Clap or say "la" for rhythm while keeping beats.
   - - Play it slowly until you get comfortable playing each note.

2. Create a game or an activity for melody.
   - Listening to the melody of a song.
   - - Guess which song the melody sounds.
   - - Sing the song to feel the flow of melody.
   - - Draw a line of flow (going up, down, or repeat) in the air with a finger or on paper.

   - Playing a musical instrument.
   - - Improvise a simple melodic pattern.
   - - Make a melodic pattern on a xylophone or other pitched instrument.
   - - Play the melodic pattern and repeat several times.
   - - My melodic pattern:

   - My idea for a game or an activity.

4-2. Developing Skills
4-2-(3) Harmonic Activities

Activity 4-2-(3)

1. Find ways to harmonize.
   - Learn about chords. For example:
   - The notes in the same chord group make good harmony when played together.
   - There are different chord family groups. For example, C major chord (C, E, and G), F major (F, A and C), and G major (G, B, and D).

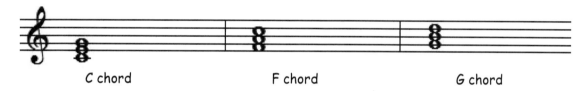

C chord   F chord   G chord

   - Play the chords using different musical instruments.
   - With an autoharp, you can press the chord button and strum the strings
   - With pitched musical instruments, find three notes that belong to the same chord group and play those together.

2. Harmonize
   - Accompany children's songs by playing chords. For example:

Twin - kle   Twin - kle   Lit - tle   Star   How   I   won - der

   - A group plays the melody while other groups play one of the chords.
   - One group of students can play percussion to keep the beat.
   - The following table is an example.

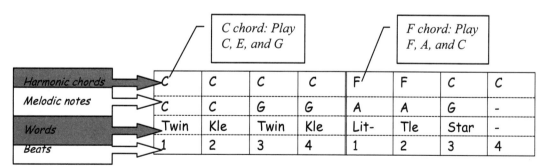

	C chord: Play C, E, and G				F chord: Play F, A, and C		
Harmonic chords	C	C	C	C	F	F	C	C
Melodic notes	C	C	G	G	A	A	G	-
Words	Twin	Kle	Twin	Kle	Lit-	Tle	Star	-
Beats	1	2	3	4	1	2	3	4

4-3. Experiencing
4-3-(1) Pitch & Melody in Music

Activity 4-3-(1)

1. Play a melody on a xylophone or any other keyboard instrument.
   - Create a melodic pattern and play it. For example:
   - Steps up such as C-D, C-D-E, etc.
   - Skips up such as C-E-G, C-G-C (high), etc.
   - Steps down such as G-F-E, C-B-A, etc.
   - Skips down such as C (high)-G, etc.
   - Repeats C-C, C-CC, etc.
   - Combination of above such as: C-E-G-F-D-D
   - My melodic motive:

   - Combine motive and make a melodic pattern. For example:
   - Repeat the melodic motive several times
   - Play one motive after another
   - Combined melodic pattern:

   - Share your feeling about your melody.

2. Listen to a piece of music, focusing on melody.
   - Listen to the music from a different culture
   - Does it have dominating notes (played more often)?
   - Is there any repeated melodic pattern?

   - Hum the melody.

4-3. Experiencing
4-3-(2) Melody and Harmony in Music

Activity 4-3-(2)

1. Listen to musical pieces played in harmony.
   - Search for music played in harmony. For example:
   - Piano trio (Piano, Violin, & Cello)
   - Singing in duet or chorus
   - My search: *Barbeshop quartet*

   - Compare the music of different combinations. For example:
   - Piano solo vs. Piano trio
   - Singing in solo vs. singing in duet
   - Acappella vs. singing with instrumental accompaniment
   - Male vs. female singing voices in harmony
   - My search: *Orchestra vs single instrument*

2. Share your feeling and thoughts with others.
   - Listening to harmonized music
   - How is each musical piece harmonized?
   - How do you feel when you listen to harmonized music?

   - In teaching children in a classroom.
   - How can we use harmonized music in class for children?
   - What are the concerns in integrating melody and/or harmony?

Reflection on Unit 4

1. At this juncture, what is your personal definition of:
   - Pitch
   - Melody
   - Harmony

2. What musical activities will you use in the classroom to:
   - Explore high or low sounds of musical instruments and/or music
   - Make melody
   - Harmonize a song

3. My reflection on the musical experience in Unit 4.
   - With respect to my personal learning and growth
   - In terms of my future teaching experience

Activities such as having the children make animal sounds and using instruments such as handbells will help the children identify whether a sound is high or low. To make melody the children can sing simple songs + listen to tapes. There are some computer software games that help children compose melody + play it back to them. To harmonize the children can sing rounds. For older children there are songs such as carols that can be sung in two part harmony.

I extended my knowledge of musical terms and the written staff. How to read notes and learned a new term - ledger lines. I think that from the instruments that we played in class the chime bars or bells

A pitch can go up, down, or stay in the same position.
However, the flow of the sound makes a melody...
and a harmony with others flow.

are the easiest for young children because you can separate the notes and have the children play one or two at a time. Together they can make chords.

Unit 5: Moving to Music

Eurhythmics
*

Harmonious and expressive movement

.

We can learn music through movement.

Movement
*

Motion

.

Musical movement includes…
music motion of playing
Or
body motion of dancing

.

Children learn basic movement
in a musical context

Unit 5
Moving to Music

You will learn and reflect on music and teaching through:

5-1. Building Knowledge

5-1-(1) Movement and Music
5-1-(2) Children's Motor Development

5-2. Developing Skills

5-2-(1) Body Parts
5-2-(2) Space
5-2-(3) Timing
5-2-(4) Quality

5-3. Experiencing

5-3-(1) Movement with Music
5-3-(2) Movement for Music (Dalcroze Method)

5-1. Building Knowledge
5-1-(1) Movement and Music

Activity 5-1-(1)

1. Relationship between music and movement.
   - Discuss the relationship between music and movement. For example:
   - Music is a movement in time. In other words, in music, a pitch moves up or down quickly/slowly, stays long or short, or so forth.
   - Children learn basic movement and choreographic skills in musical/rhythmic contexts.[1] Children learn what and how to move responding to music.
   - My thoughts:

2. Aspects of Movement.
   - What are the aspects of movement?
   - What we move: Body Parts
   - Where we move: Space
   - When we move: Timing
   - How we move: Quality

   - How does music affect each aspect of movement? For example:
   - Music effects motivate movement of body parts (see 5-2)
   - Tempo of music can influence how fast you move (timing).
   - Dynamics of music can give an idea of how to move (quality).
   - My thoughts:

---

[1] Consortium of National Arts Education Associations. (1994). *National Standards for Arts Education: What Every Young American Should Know and Be Able to Do in the Arts*. VA: Music Educators National Conference.

5-1. Building Knowledge
5-1-(2) Children's Motor Development

Activity 5-1-(2)

1. Children's motor development
   - Research children's motor development. For example[1]:
   - 8 month-1 year: Walks in a wide stance like a waddle
   - 1-2 years: Walks in a toddle and uses arms for balance
   - 2-3 years: Walks up stairs; Runs stiffly, has difficulty turning corners and stopping quickly; Jumps off bottom step with both feet
   - 3-4 years: Walks with arms swinging; Walks straight line; Runs more smoothly; Has more control over starting and stopping
   - 4-5 years: Walks circular line; Skips with one foot; Gallops; Walks balance beam; Displays strong, speedy running; Turns corners, starts and stops easily; Jumps up, down, and forward
   - 5-6 years: Walks as an adult; Skips with alternating feet; Shows mature running; Displays increased speed and control
   - My research: *center of gravity changes from head in babies to abdomen in toddler + feet in young children.*

2. Children's motor development and musical development
   - Discuss how children's motor development can be considered in musical activities. For example, when planning the movement activities for 4, 5 years:
   - Consider tempo of music for speed of movement
   - Try movement in different ways such as jumping, skipping, or galloping
   - My thoughts: *Four elements in movement :-*

cephal
proximal distal   *pincer grasp.*

---

[1] Schickedanze, J. A., Schickedanze, D. I., Forsyth, P. D., & Forsyth, G. A (2001). 'Physical Development in Preschool Children,' Ch. 8 of the Book, *Understanding Children and Adolescents*. MA: Allyn and Bacon.

5-2. Developing Skills
5-2-(1) Body Parts

Activity 5-2-(1)

1. Explore the movement of body parts.
   - Brainstorm which body parts you can move. For example:
   - Parts in face: eyes, eyebrows, lips, etc.
   - Parts in arms: fingers, wrists, etc.
   - More body parts:
     Shoulders, elbows

   - Share how you can move body parts. For example:
   - Different movement with feet: walk, run, slide, gallop, skip, hop, jump, etc.
   - Arms & legs: bend, stretch, extend, etc.
   - More ideas:

2. Relate music to body movements.
   - Explore different musical pieces and find ways to use music to move different body parts. For example:
   - Music effects[1] (short piece of music in different style for special effect) may motivate to move certain body parts.
   - Different rhythms of music help you to move in different ways such as walking, stretching, and so forth.
   - My search:

   - Think of some ways you can use each musical piece you've researched for body movement.

---

[1] Madacy Music Group. (1994). *Music Effects* Vol.1 Quebec, Canada: Distributions Madacy Inc.

5-2. Developing Skills
5-2-(2) Space

Activity 5-2-(2)

1. Discuss how you can move using different space.

Space	Movements
Place	• Staying in one place • Travel from one place to another
Direction	• Forward/Backward • Right/Left • Up/Down
Level	• High/Middle/Low • Over/Under
Shape	• Curve, Straight line, Angle

2. Make a musical game or plan an activity through which your students can experience different spaces.
   - You can relate a musical concept with a way of moving in space. For example:
   - Move in different level (high, middle, or low) according to the sound in different pitches (high, middle, or low) of musical instruments.
   - My idea:

   Pitch – high + low movements
   Use different types of music to promote different types of movement

   - You can use different types of music or musical instruments for different movements. For example,
   - Walking along with a drum beat, children can change the direction whenever they hear a bell ringing, and so forth.
   - My idea:

5-2. Developing Skills
5-2-(3) Timing

Activity 5-2-(3)

1. Discuss how you can move differently in terms of timing.

Time	Movements
Tempo	• Fast/Slow • Fast to slow/gradually speedy
Duration	• Brief to long duration
Accents	• Occurring in predictable intervals • Occurring in unpredictable intervals
Rhythm and Beats	• 2, 3, 4 beats, etc.

2. Make one or two musical games or plan an activity on timing of movement.
    *   You can match the timing of movement to the timing of music. For example:
    -   Walk around a circle with a drum playing (beat).
    -   Match the speed of your walk to the speed of a drum beat (tempo).
    -   Walk around while music plays. Stop walking when the music stops (duration)
    -   Change the direction when you hear the sound of a certain instrument such as cymbals (accent)

    *   Discuss how you can move and/or play instruments differently to reflect elements of timing such as tempo, duration, accents, or beat and rhythm. For example:
    -   Movement of accent: change direction, lift hands up, clap, jump, etc.
    -   Instrument to play accents: cymbals, gong, triangle, etc.
    -   My idea:

3. Research musical recordings to be used for movement in different tempos, rhythms, and beats.

5-2. Developing Skills
5-2-(4) Quality

Activity 5-2-(4)

1. Brainstorm different expressions in terms of quality of movement.

Quality	Movements	
Energy	Strong, Light, Soft, etc.	*dynamic*
Feeling	Joyful, Sad, etc.	*tempo - key*
Images	Fallen leaves, etc.	*high to low pitch*
Themes	With a story such as *Peter and the wolf*, etc.	

2. Research musical pieces you can use for the quality of movement.
    - Musical pieces with thematic titles can help to present different feelings, images, ideas, or themes. For example:
    - Dan Gibson's "Forest Piano"[1]
    - Mussorgsky, "Pictures at an Exhibition"[2]
    - Rimsky-Korsakov, "Flight of the Bumblebee"[3]
    - Saint-Saengs, "Carnival of Animals"[4]
    - Prokofiev, "Peter and the Wolf"[5]
    - Tchaikovsky, "Nutcracker Suite"[6]
    - My search:

    - Music played in different tempos and/or dynamics help to present different feelings, images, ideas, or themes. For instance:
    - Music played quietly can be expressed softly in movement.
    - Music played in high pitch can be expressed brightly in the movement.
    - My thought:

---

[1] Dan Gibson (1996). *Forest Piano; Exploring Nature With Music*. Toronto, Canada: Solitudes Ltd.
[2] Volgograd Philharmonic Orchestra & Edward Serov (1995). *Mussorgsky: Pictures at an Exhibition*. Amadis, HNH International Ltd.
[3] Yo-Yo Ma & Bobby McFerrin. (1992). Yo-Yo Ma Bobby McFerrin Hush. New York: Sony Music Entertainment Inc.
[4] Boston Pops Orchestra. (1988). *Classics for Children*. New York: BMG Music.
[5] Boston Pops Orchestra. (1988). *Classics for Children*. New York: BMG Music.
[6] Boston Pops Orchestra. (1998). *Classics for Children*. New York: BMG Music.

5-3. Experiencing
5-3-(1) Movement with Music

Activity 5-3-(1)

1. Personal Dance[1]
   - Discuss why we dance. For example:
   - Personal dance emphasizes the development of perception, creativity, and self-expression as well as physical coordination and control.[2]
   - My thought:

   - Search resources of personal dance. For example[3]:
   - India: Bharata natyam- Classical dance: "A devotional dance to Shiva"
   - Korea: "Salpuri", traditional dance of spirit
   - My search:

   - Watching a personal dance, share your observation on how the dancer moves differently with musical changes.
   - Moving body parts:
   - Using different space:
   - Moving timing:
   - Quality of movement:

   - Share your ideas on what children can do related to personal dance.
   - Draw a pose of movement in the video
   - Dance with scarves, ribbons, and so forth
   - Express an animal through movement.
   - My idea:

---

[1] Personal Dance refers to a dance of one person.
[2] Little, A. (Project Director). (1977). Dance as Education. Washington, D.C.: National Dance Association, an Association of the American Alliance for Health, Physical Education and Recreation.
[3] The JVC Video Anthology of Word Music and Dance. Japan: Victor Company.

2. Social Dance[1]
   - Search resources of dance in which you can find folk dance from different countries.[2] For example:
     - Ireland: Folk dance with concertina accompaniment
     - France: Farandole-Folk dance
     - Spain: Folk dance: "Bolero de Belmar"
     - Greece: Pentozali-Folk dance from Crete
     - Soviet Union, Mari (Autonomous Republic): Folk dance and folk song
     - My search:

   - Discuss the similarities and differences among folk dances.
     - Music
     - Form and shape
     - My observation:

   - Make a folk dance in a group.
     - Shape: In a circle, square, or line
     - Song or music used:
     - Movement: how and when to move.
     - My group's choreography:

   - Share your thoughts and feeling. For example:
     - In choreographing to plan the shapes of the movement, body movement, etc.
     - Thinking of what children can do to participate.
     - My thoughts and/or feeling:

     Express thoughts sadness, happiness
     symbolic, religious dance
     etc work alone or with partner
     folk dancing
     ballet
     line dancing

---

[1] Social Dance refers to a dance by more than two people in a structured form.
[2] The JVC Video Anthology of Word Music and Dance. Japan: Victor Company.

3. Cultural Dance[1]
    *   Search resources such as video in which you can see cultural dance.[2] For example:
    -   Mexico: Dance with mariachi [string and brass] ensemble: "Jarabe Tapatio" (Mexican hat dance)
    -   American Indians of the Plateau Region: War dance, Hoop dance, Rabbit dance.
    -   Korea: T'alch'um-masked dance-drama from the Pongsan region
    -   Mali: Masked dance of the Dogon
    -   Zaire: Dance of the Bambuti
    -   England: Sword dance of Scottish soldiers
    -   My search:

    *   Share your thoughts and feeling. For example:
    -   How culture (ethnic origins, their aesthetic principles, and so forth) is reflected in dances
    -   How the mood of music matches to cultural dance.
    -   My thought and/or feeling:

---

[1] Cultural Dance refers to a dance that reflects particular periods or cultures. It can be either personal or social dance.
[2] The JVC Video Anthology of Word Music and Dance. Japan: Victor Company.

5-3. Experiencing
5-3-(2) Movement for Music (Dalcroze Method)

Activity 5-3-(2)

1. Feel the movement of music.
   - Listen to a musical piece and try to feel how music moves. For example:
   - How it moves up or down
   - How fast/slow it moves.
   - My listening:

   - Share what you feel. For example:
   - How the movement of music changes the mood
   - How the movement of music makes me want to move (or dance).
   - My feeling:

2. Research music teaching method, focusing on learning music through movement.
   - Research on *Dalcroze method.*[1]
   - Dalcroze method is a system of musical education developed by Emile Jaques-Dalcroze (1865-1950).
   - The method is based on the idea of experiencing music and developing musical abilities through rhythmic movement.
   - The system has three components: eurhythmics, solfege[2](with "fixed do"), and improvisation at the piano.[3]
   - My search:

   - Focus on *Eurhythmics* and explain it. For example:
   - Harmonious and expressive movement[4]
   - My explanation:

3. Discuss about how you can use 'Eurhythmics.'
   - Find ways to integrate Eurythmics in teaching musical concepts.
   - Walk around with music in different tempos to learn tempos of music.
   - Draw a line in the air while listening to music to learn pitch and melody.
   - My idea:

---

[1] Robert M. Abramson. (1992). *Dalcroze Eurhythmics.* IL: GIA Publications, Inc.
[2] The term "solfege" will be focused more in the next unit.
[3] Randel, D. M. (ed.). (1986). *The New Harvard Dictionary of Music.* MA: The Belknap Press of Harvard University Press
[4] Choksy, L., Abramson, R., Gillespie, A., & Wood, D. (1986) *Teaching music in the twentieth century.* Englewood Cliffs, NJ: Prentice Hall, Inc.

Reflection on Unit 5

1. At this juncture, what is your personal definition of:
   - Musical movement
   - Eurythmics

2. What musical activities will you use in the classroom to:
   - Explore body parts through musical movement
   - Move using different space
   - Move differently in terms of timing
   - Express using different qualities of movement

3. My reflection on the musical experience in Unit 5.
   - With respect to my personal learning and growth
   - In terms of my future teaching experience

To explore body parts through movement it is good to use a wide variety of musical genres and also through the use of different dynamics, tempos and pitch to move in different planes + shapes + speeds. The children could be elephants to loud, slow tempo music + gazelles to light, fast, music. The music or beat that is chosen can be used to tell a story such as a caterpillar turning into a butterfly or a train running slow then faster down a track.

Sometimes in the classroom I think it is good to let the children listen and interpret the music without giving pre-set ideas. This will help increase their vocabulary as they try to describe either how they felt or what the music made them think of. As the children get used to making rhythms with the instruments a good activity would be to ask the children how they think a certain ___ would sound on an instrument (such as rain) and then have one half play + the others interpret the movements. In the classroom, before the lesson, I have used different types of music for different movement but I realized from the activities that pitch and dynamics are also important + will try these exercises. For example singing + moving fast + loud or quiet + slow to

> *Movement of music helps you feel emotion in music and it helps you express your emotion while moving to the music.*

Unit 6: Singing Music

I know an old lady
Who swallowed a bird,
How absurd,
She swallowed a bird!
She swallowed the bird
To catch the spider...

3

Songs such as "head shoulders, knees + toes"
+ "row the boat"

Singing

*

Common form of making music with the voice

Use words (not humming)

Solfege

*

Textless vocal exercises

.

We can learn music
through the use of the voice as a musical instrument

Unit 6
Singing

You will learn and reflect on music and teaching through:

6-1. Building Knowledge

6-1-(1) Singing
6-1-(2) Children's Vocal Development

6-2. Developing Skills

6-2-(1) Singing for Fun
6-2-(2) Singing to Express Feelings
6-2-(3) Singing to Learn
6-2-(4) Singing in Diversity

6-3. Experiencing

6-3-(1) Feeling Music in Singing
6-3-(2) Singing for Music (Kodaly Method)

6-1. Building Knowledge
6-1-(1) Singing and Music

Activity 6-1-(1)

1. Define Singing in your own words.
    - You can research the term in music dictionaries and explain it in your own words. For example:
      - Singing is the most common form of music making. It is the use of the voice as a musical instrument with the mouth open (as distinct from humming).[1]
      - My definition:

2. Discuss why singing is meaningful in our lives.
    - Share your experiences with singing. For example:
      - When, where, what, and why you sing
      - How you feel when you sing
      - My experience of singing:

    - Discuss why we sing. For example:
      - Singing gives joy
      - Singing gives entertainment when people get together.
      - My thought: Express heritage.

3. Think about the relationship between singing and music.
    - How music affects singing. For example:
      - When singing is accompanied by musical instruments, it sounds beautiful.
      - We can sing more accurately (especially in pitch) with playing music.
      - My thought:

---

[1] Randel, D. M. (ed.). (1986). *The New Harvard Dictionary of Music*. MA: The Belknap Press of Harvard University Press

6-1. Building Knowledge
6-1-(2) Children's Vocal Development

Activity 6-1-(2)

1. Research children's vocal development.
   - Children's vocalization stage[1]
   - Birth-3 months: The first vocalization *crying + cooing*
   - 3 months-1½ years: Vocal experimentation and sound imitation *babbling (reduplicative / proto words)*
   - 1½-3 years: Approximation of singing
   - 3-4 years: Singing accuracy in limited range *limited pitch*
   - After 4 years: Singing accuracy with expanded range.

   - Factors influencing children's vocal development.[2] For example:
   - Internal factors: Age, gender, or other genetic factor.
   - External Factors: Personal or instrumental stimulation through modeling or accompanying

   - Children's development related to singing. For example[3]:
   - 12-14 months: Vocal play, experimentation with sound.
   - 19 months: Melodic and rhythmic patterns appearing in vocalizations
   - 19-24 months: Free experimentation with songs; short spontaneous songs, often consisting of a small melodic interval with a flexible rhythm pattern.
   - 2 years: Use of melodic patterns from learned songs in spontaneous singing. Ability to sing parts of songs.
   - 2½- 3 years: Imitation of songs, though rarely with total accuracy.
   - 4 years: Sequence followed in learning songs: words, rhythm, phrases, melodic contour.
   - 5-5½ years: Sense of key stabilized; can sing most songs when learned fairly accurately.
   - My search:

2. Discuss how we should apply the research results to teaching music.

---

[1] Greenberg, M. (1979). *Your Children Need Music*. NJ: Prentice-Hall, Inc.
[2] Kim, J. (1998). Effects of Word Type, Context, and Vocal Assistance on Children's Pitch-Matching Abilities: An Early Childhood Educator's View. *Doctoral dissertation*. Teachers College, Columbia University.
[3] McDonald, D. T., & Simons, G. M. (1989). *Musical Growth and Development: Birth through Six*. New York: Shirmer Books.

6-2. Developing Skills
6-2-(1) Singing for Fun

Activity 6-2-(1)

1. Learn children's songs for fun.
    *   Search for children's songs on websites, songbooks, etc. For example:
    -   *The Silly Songbook*[1]
    -   *The Funny Songbook*[2]
    -   My search:

    *   Learn and sing some of those songs.
    -   Some of them, called silly songs, have no meaning but the words are funny.
    -   While singing some of them, you have simple finger motions called "finger plays" while singing.
    -   The song I learned:

2. Discuss why those songs are meaningful for children.
    *   What are some advantages of singing songs for fun, from an educational perspective? For example:
    -   Fun to sing. In other words, children get joy out of singing with others.
    -   Easy to learn. Since those songs have simple melodic and/or rhythmic patterns, children can follow and learn songs easily.
    -   Helpful for children's development. Some songs come with finger-plays children can follow and improve their motor-development skills. Some songs teach words or concepts so that children can learn or memorize certain concepts through singing repeated verses.
    -   Convenient for teachers because, even with no visual materials, children give their attention
    -   My thought:

    *   What are some weaknesses of singing silly songs? For example:
    -   Words in some of those songs are different from reality, and even violent in some cases.
    -   My thought:

---

[1] Nelson, E. (1984). *The Silly Songbook,* New York: Sterling Publishing Co., Inc.
[2] Nelson, E. (1984). *The Funny Songbook,* New York: Sterling Publishing Co., Inc.

6-2. Developing Skills
6-2-(2) Singing to Express Feelings

Activity 6-2-(2)

1. Discuss how some songs express our mood/feeling through poetic words or story.
    *   Think about what might be a three-year-old child's feeling presented in the following song.

<u>Dragon Song</u>
Words and Chant by Clara

I thought it was a real dragon...I thought it was real
But it was not...It was not.
I'm not afraid of it any more ... No! No! ... I'm not afraid of it any more.

    *   Research children's songs with poetic words or stories. Then, discuss how writers express feelings through the words of those songs.
    -   My search and thought:

2. Discuss the relationship between music and words in songs.
    *   Read the words only and then sing the words in a song. How is it different?
    *   Sing the same words in different tunes (singing "twinkle twinkle" in tune of other songs, for example.) How does it change the mood of a song?
    *   Why is it important for words to be partnered with appropriate music?
    -   My thought and feeling:

3. Discuss some ways of using and/or teaching expressive children's songs in a classroom setting.
    *   Teaching expressive songs. For example:
    -   Watching a performance from an opera or a musical and discussing how singers express feeling through singing.
    -   Listening to a song and guessing the feeling of writers.
    -   My idea: Let them pick the song Based on weather or holiday.
    *   Making expressive songs. For example:
    -   After a field trip, write a poem together and make up a song.
    -   My idea:

6-2. Developing Skills
6-2-(3) Singing to Learn

Activity 6-2-(3)

1. Research children's songs.
   - Review children's songs from songbooks. For example:
   - "Wee Sing" series[1]
   - "Music for Very Little People"[2]
   - My search:

   - Research websites for children's songs. For example:
   - http://www.kididdles.com/museum contains downloadable songs for children
   - http://www.bestchildrensmusic.com has a library of children's music
   - My search:

   - Research records of children's songs. Some examples of records by famous children's song writers are:
   - Hap Palmer[3]
   - Ella Jenkins[4]
   - Raffi"[5]
   - My search:

2. Categorize children's songs in terms of different concepts or themes.
   - Songs for different occasions.
   - Seasons of Spring, Summer, Fall, and Winter:
   - Holidays such as Christmas, etc.:

   - Songs of different aspects of nature
   - Insects/Animals: *Itsy Bitsy Spider – Five little Ducks / Five little monkeys*
   - Flowers/Trees: *Green grass grows*
   - Stars/Sky: *Twinkle twinkle*
   - Other categories:

---

[1] Beall, P. C., & Nipp, S. H. (1985). *Wee Sing/ Wee Sing and Play/ Wee Sing Silly Song/ Wee Sing Around the Campfire*. Los Angeles, CA: Price/Stern/Sloan Publishers, Inc.
[2] Feierabend, J. M. (1986). *Music for Very Little People*. Farmingdale, NY: Boosey Hawkes, Inc.
[3] Palmer, Hap. *Baby Songs(AR713)/ Feelin' Free (AR 517)*. Freeport, NY: Aducational Activities, Inc.
[4] Jenkins, Ella. *And One and Two (FC7544)/ Call-and-Response Rhythmic Group Singing (FC7638)/ Early Childhood Songs (FC7630)/ Songs and Rhythms from Near and Far (FC7655)/ This-A-Way, That-A-Way: Cheerful Songs and Chants (FC7546)/ You'll Sing a Song and I'll Sing a Song (FC 7664)*. NY: Folkways Records.
[5] Raffi. *Rise and Shine*. Troubadour Records Ltd.

- Songs of different objects
  - Kitchen: "I'm A Little Teapot"
  - Transportation: "The Bus," etc. *Down by The Station*
  - And more...:

- Songs for exploring myself
  - Feeling: "If You're Happy"
  - Body parts: 'Where Is Thumbkin?" "Head, Shoulder, Knees, and Toes," *Hokey Pokey*
  - And more...:

- Songs for learning words
  - Alphabet: "ABC" (in a tune of "Twinkle Twinkle Little Star"),
  - Days: "There Are Seven Days" (in a tune of "Oh My darling, Clementine")
  - And more...:

3. Make games or activities to learn concepts in singing.
   - Compose a song or words of a song. For example:
     - Using the same melody, write the words on different themes or certain concepts.
     - Write a song to memorize certain concepts.
     - My idea:

   - Singing songs. For example:
     - Sing the songs we know on a certain theme (such as animals)
     - Take turns singing songs on a certain theme
     - My idea:

6-2. Developing Skills of Singing
6-2-(4) Singing in Diversity

Activity 6-2-(4)

1. Sing songs in different styles of music
    *   You may find some familiar songs from records or videotapes.[1] For example:
    -   Folk Songs: Old Kentucky Home, Swanee River, I Dream of Jeanie, Dixieland, Oh Susannah, House of the Rising Sun, Old House', and so forth.
    -   Country Songs: "Wagon Wheels," and so forth.
    -   Jazz: "When the Saints Go Marching In," and so forth.
    -   Rock & Roll: "Old Time Rock & Roll" "Charlie Brown" and so forth.
    -   Gospel: "Oh Happy Day," and so forth.

    *   Discuss how those styles can be reflected in children's music.
    -   You can sing the same words of a song in different styles.
    -   We can use the music of songs in different style in a daily schedule for background music, movement, etc.

2. Sing songs from other cultures.[2]
    *   Learn different songs from different cultures. For example, listen to the words below.

Paeng-E

By Jinyoung Kim

Paeng, Paeng, Paeng-E-ga...Jal Do-ra-ga-da-ga
Beatle, Beatle Geo-ri-deo-ni...Noo-wa-beo-ryut-nae.

    *   Share how you learned songs.
    -   We can find some syllables similar to the language we're using (e.g., beetle)
    -   We can memorize simple and repeated syllables and/or rhythm (e.g., Paeng)

    *   Discuss how you can teach the songs to children.
    -   Let the children find similar sounds and sing that part only in the beginning of the song.
    -   Teach different words gradually.
    -   My idea:

---

[1] The Bennett Group. (1994). "America's Music" Series. CA: A Bennett Group.
[2] http://www.mamalisa.com has children's songs and lyrics from around the world.

3. Sing songs in different combinations of people.
   - Learn how we call different combinations of people in singing.
     - *Solo*: A person sings alone.
     - *Duet*: Two people sing together.
     - *Chorus*: A body of singers who perform together, either in unison or in parts, usually with more than one on a part.

   - Learn the names of different vocal parts.
     - *Soprano*: The highest-pitched human voice, normally by women
     - *Alto*: A low female voice
     - *Tenor*: The highest voice by male.
     - *Bass*: The lowest voice by male.
     - My search: Identify singers you know from each vocal part.

   - Create some activities in which your students can sing in different combinations.

4. Sing songs with different instrumental accompaniment.
   - Review the types of musical instruments (see Unit 1).
   - Discuss how you can use different musical instruments in singing children's songs (see Unit 7).

6-3. Experiencing
6-3-(1) Feeling Music in Singing

Activity 6-3-(1)

1. Timbre in Singing.
   - Learn the following song.

<u>What is it?</u>
Music and words by Jinyoung Kim

You blow it
It is brass
Has three keys
Trumpet

Beat	1	2	3	4	1	2	3	4
Melody	D'	D'	D'	-	A'	D"	A'	-
Words	It	Is	Big	-	What	Is	It	?
(Words	Black	And	White	-				
to	Many	Many	Boards	-				
repeat)	Play	With	Fingers	-				
Beat	1	2	3	4	1	2	3	4
Melody	A'		A'	A'	D'			
	It	-	Is	A	Piano	-	-	-

- Count one, two, three, (and) four for each column in your mind to keep a steady beat.
- To sing, you only need 3 different notes: E and 2 As-one lower and the other higher than E. Find and play these three notes on a Xylophone or other pitched musical instruments.
- Every line, except the last line, has the same melody.
- Sing the song. You can take a turn: the first 4 beats sung by a person (or a group) and the next 4 beats sung by another.
- The last line is sung by the second person (group) who has sung the "what is it?" part. If this person guessed a wrong instrument, the first person sings the same part one more time with the right (intended) answer.

   - Discuss other ways of using the song to explore Timbre. For example:
- Make different words for different musical instruments.
- In the first set of 4 beats, instead of singing the words, you can sing "It sounds…" and play the musical instrument so that the other group can guess by listening to the sound of musical instruments.
- My idea:

2. Beat and Measure in Singing
   - Sing the following two songs.
   - Two songs have the same words and the same melody line. However, the beat of one song is different from the other.
   - Count one and two for the first song, one, two, and three for the second song.
   - In the first song, you play each note for "I" and "Can" once in each beat. However, for "Do-It," you play the note twice in a beat. In other words, you play each note for a half beat so that you can play two notes evenly in a beat.
   - In the second song, don't forget taking a rest in the second beat after singing "I" and "It" to keep steady 3 beats.

I Can Do It (2/4)
By Jinyoung Kim

Beat	1	2	1	2	1	2	1	2
Words (Melody)	I (C')	Can (C')	Do-It (C' C')	-	I (D')	Can (D')	Do-It (D' D')	-
Words (Melody)	I (E')	Can (E')	Do-It (F' F')	-	By (E')	My- (D')	self (C')	-

I Can Do It (3/4)
By Jinyoung Kim

1	2	3	1	2	3	1	2	3	1	2	3
I (C')	-	Can (C')	Do (C')	It (C')	-	I (D')	-	Can (D')	Do (D')	It (D')	-
I (E')	-	Can (E')	Do (F')	It (F')	-	Wi- (E')	th -	My (D')	Frie- (C')	nds -	-

- Share how you feel differently singing the same song in two different beats.

- Sing other children's songs in the measure of 2/4, 3/4, or 4/4.

3. Pitch in Singing
   - Learn the following song.
   - For this song, you need 5 different notes: E, F, G, A, and C (high). You can use hand bells or play on a xylophone for the notes.
   - Each note matches for each direction: C" (high) is for Up, E for Down, F for Front, A for Back, and G for Side.
   - Count one, two, three, (and) four in your head so that you can sing the song in a steady beat.

<u>Up, Down…</u>

By Jinyoung Kim

1	2	3	4	1	2	3	4
Up (C")	Up (C")	Up (C")	-	Down (E')	Down (E')	Down (E')	-
Front (F')	Back (A')	Front (F')	Back (A')	Side (G')	Side (G')	Side (G')	-
Up (C")	Up (C")	Up (C")	-	Down (E')	Down (E')	Down (E')	-
Front (F')	Back (A')	Front (F')	Back (A')	Side (G')	Side (G')	Side (G')	-
You can (A')	Point it (A')	Any- (A')	where (A')	With (G')	Your (G')	Fin- (G')	gers (G')
Up (C")	-	Down (E')	-	Front (F')	Back (A')	Side (G')	-

   - When you get familiar with the song, you can make a pitch game.
   - At the end of the song, a person plays one of five notes and others guess what it is.
   - Sing the words the first time. Then, gradually remove the words and just point the direction so that you can listen to each pitch clearly.

   - Discuss some other ways of using the song for children. For example:
   - Children can name what they can see when they point in each direction.
   - When the teacher points in each direction, children can sing out or play each pitch, or vice versa.
   - My idea:

4. Melody and Harmony in Singing

- Learn the following song.
- Divide into 3 different groups.
- The first group begins the song. After the 3 beat, the second group begins the song. Then, after 3 more beats, the third group begins the song.

One Body
By Jinyoung Kim

1	2	3	1	2	3	1	2	3
Mouth (C')	Mouth (C')	Mouth (C')	Head (G')	Head (G')	Head (G')	Eyes (E')	Eyes (E')	Eyes (E')
			Mouth (C')	Mouth (C')	Mouth (C')	Head (G')	Head (G')	Head (G')
						Mouth (C')	Mouth (C')	Mouth (C')
Head (G')	Head (G')	Head (G')	Ears (F')	Ears (F')	Ears (F')	Nose (D')	Nose (D')	Nose (D')
Eyes (E')	Eyes (E')	Eyes (E')	Head (G')	Head (G')	Head (G')	Ears (F')	Ears (F')	Ears (F')
Head (G')	Head (G')	Head (G')	Eyes (E')	Eyes (E')	Eyes (E')	Head (G')	Head (G')	Head (G')
All (G')	Is (G')	One (G')	Bo- (E')	dy (C')	- / -			
Nose (D')	Nose (D')	Nose (D')	All (G')	Is (G')	One (G')	Bo- (E')	dy (C')	- / -
Ears (F')	Ears (F')	Ears (F')	Nose (D')	Nose (D')	Nose (D')	All (G')	Is (G')	One (G')
Bo- (E')	dy (C')	- / -						

Group 1 →

Group 2 →

Group 3 →

6-3. Experiencing
6-3-(2) Singing for Music (Kodaly Method)

Activity 6-3-(2)

1. Research methods to learn music through singing.
    - Research the Kodaly method.
    - The Kodaly method was developed by the Hungarian composer Zoltan Kodaly (1882-1967).
    - The objective of the Kodaly Method is the development of music literacy: the ability to read, write, and think music.
    - He devised a series of speech syllables for rhythmic instruction, with a different syllable for each note value.
    - The method follows sequential presentation of materials. Songs selected for singing instruction and melodic study are sequenced for presentation according to the pitches they contain.
    - My research:

    - Research on *Solfege*
    - *Solfege* is a textless vocal exercise (first Italian, later also French) in the 17th century and subsequently.
    - My research:

2. Discuss how you can use the Kodaly method in your teaching.
    - Follow a teaching direction[1] of the Kodaly method. For example:
    - Learn a song by imitating the teacher.
    - Step the beat while singing the song.
    - Sing the song, clapping the rhythm of the words.
    - Sing the song alternating between clapping the beat and the word rhythm.
    - Identify the higher tones "sol" and lower tones "mi." learn hand signs for "sol" and "mi."
    - Sing the song using hand signs.
    - Show the rhythmic notation for the song.
    - Show the melodic notation for the song, perhaps on an abbreviated staff.

    - Share your feeling and thoughts in using the Kodaly method.

---

[1] Choksy, L. (1981). *The Kodaly Context*. Englewood Cliffs, NJ: Prentice-Hall, Inc.

Reflection on Unit 6

1. At this juncture, what is your personal definition of:
    *   Singing

2. What musical activities will you use in the classroom to:
    *   Sing for fun
    *   Sing to express feelings
    *   Sing to learn concepts
    *   Sing the songs of different cultures

3. My reflection on the musical experience in Unit 6.
    *   With respect to my personal learning and growth
    *   In terms of my future teaching experience

*I may not be able to carry a tune,
but I can still enjoy singing.*

Unit 7: Playing Music

Ostinato
*

An elemental structural device
It persistently repeats a pattern or motive

.

We can use it to learn music
repeating patterns over and over

Playing
*

We play musical instruments
to play or to accompany others

Unit 7
Playing Music

You will learn and reflect on music and teaching through:

7-1. Building Knowledge

7-1-(1) Playing and Music
7-1-(2) Children's Development

7-2. Developing Skills

7-2-(1) Playing to Accompany
7-2-(2) Playing to Teach

7-3. Experiencing

7-3-(1) Playing Music Together
7-3-(2) Playing for Music (Orff Method)

7-1. Building Knowledge
7-1-(1) Playing and Music

Activity 7-1-(1)

1. Share your experience in the playing of music.
   - What kind of musical instruments do you play?
   - What I play:
   - How long I've played:
   - How good I am at playing:

   - What was your experience in the process of learning how to play a musical instrument?
   - What was the most difficult part in learning?
   - Did you like your music teacher when you learned how to play? Why?

   - How did the ability to play a musical instrument affect your life?
   - Did it change life, personality, or so forth?
   - Does it help when I do other things?

2. Discuss the importance of playing music in class.
   - Do classroom teachers need to play musical instruments in class? Why?

   - What are the skills (if any) teachers can develop to play in class? Why? For example:
   - Reading basic musical notes
   - Learning how to integrate musical sound into other activities
   - My thought:

7-1. Building Knowledge
7-1-(2) Children's Development

Activity 7-1-(2)

1. Research children's development of playing musical instruments.
   - Review research on children's development related to playing music. For example[1]:
   - Children are naturally interested in the use of musical instruments.
   - Children can learn many things about instruments through free exploration. However, instruction should be provided not in a conventional way but when needed at the time.
   - Experiences with instruments lead to growth in understanding timbre, pitch, melody, rhythm, and so forth.
   - My search:

2. Discuss the relationship between playing and teaching children in class.
   - Why would it be good for children to play musical instruments in class? For example:
   - To create music to express feelings
   - To play the song they like or familiar music
   - My thought:

   - Why would it be good for teachers to play musical instruments in class? For example:
   - To accompany music when children sing
   - To create musical effect in storytelling, and so forth.
   - My thought:

   - What are some ways of playing and using musical instruments in class? For example:
   - To accompany songs when singing in group time
   - To explore sound and play in music area during free play
   - My idea:

---

[1] Moorhead, G. E., & Pond, D. (1978). *Music of Young Children*. Santa Barbara, CA: Pillsbury Foundation for Advancement of Music Education.

7-2. Developing Skills
7-2-(1) Playing to Accompany

Activity 7-2-(1)

1. Review Unit 5 on pitch, melody, and harmony to be able to read musical notes.
   - Practice familiar children's songs.

   - You may want to make a table to write down the melody of the song. For example:

- Little Star

Twinkle		Twinkle		Little		Star -		How I		Wonder		What you		are	
C'	C'	G'	G'	A'	A'	G'	-	F'	F'	E'	E'	D'	D'	C'	-
Up	a-	bove the		World so		High		Like a		Diamond		In the		sky	
G'	G'	F'	F'	E'	E'	D'	-	G'	G'	F'	F'	E'	E'	D'	-
Twinkle		Twinkle		Little		Star -		How I		Wonder		What you		are	
C'	C'	G'	G'	A'	A'	G'	-	F'	F'	E'	E'	D'	D'	C'	-

- Mary Had a Little Lamb

Mary				Had a		Little		Lamb	
E'	-	-	D'	C'	D'	E'	E'	E'	-
Little				Lamb		Little		Lamb	
D'		D'		D'	-	E'	G'	G'	-
Mary				Had a		Little		Lamb It's	
E'	-	-	D'	C'	D'	E'	E'	E'	E'
Fleece is		White as		Snow				-	
D'		D'		E'	D'	C'	-	-	-

- Are You Sleeping?

Are you		Sleeping		Are you		sleeping	
C'	D'	E'	C'	C'	D'	E'	C'
Brother		John		Brother		john	
E'	F'	G'	-	E'	F'	G'	-
Morning bells are			Ringing		Morning bells are			ringing
G'	A'	G'	F'	E'	C'	G'	A'	G'	F'	E'	C'
Ding ding		Dong -		Ding ding		dong	
C'	G	C'	-	C'	G	C'	-

7-2. Developing Skills
7-2-(2) Playing to Teach

Activity 7-2-(2)

1. Make a musical game or plan an activity through which your students can learn how to play.
   - Plan a musical activity using a xylophone. For example:
   - Attach the numbers on the boards of a xylophone. Children play the last 4 digits of their telephone number or birthday, matching numbers.
   - My idea:

   - Plan a musical activity using musical symbols. For example:
   - Play a xylophone or a keyboard, matching a simple melodic pattern drawn on a flash card.
   - My idea:

2. Make teaching materials you might need when teaching how to play musical instruments.
   - Use musical symbols in children's manipulative materials. For example:
   - A puzzle to match each note and the name of the note: For example, a written name and a drawn symbol of a quarter note
   - My idea:

   - Make visual aids for group activities. For example:
   - Flash cards with musical symbols, to be used for a game
   - Boards with different notes of a scale.

7-3. Experiencing
7-3-(1) Playing Music Together

Activity 7-3-(1)

1. Learn a new song.
    *   On a Xylophone, Metalophone, or Glockenspiel, find C, D, E, G, and A.
    -   Leave those keys only and remove all other keys.
    -   Play C and G with two mallets (sticks to bang) in consistent 4 beats.

    *   Learn the following song.

I Can Play the Xylophone
Words and Music by Jinyoung Kim

I can play the xy - lop-phone   You can play the   xy - lo-phone   Lis -ten to

What I play   Let me hear   what you play

-   To read the notes, you may want to draw a table in your mind.

1	2	3	4	1	2	3	4
I	Can	Play	The	Xy-	Lo-	Phone	-
C'	C'	C'	D'	E'	E'	G'	-
You	Can	Play	The	Xy-	Lo-	Phone	-
C'	C'	C'	D'	E'	E'	G'	-
Lis-	Ten	To	-	What	I	Play	-
A'	A'	G'	-	A'	A'	G'	-
Let	Me	Hear	-	What	You	Play	-
A'	A'	G'	-	E'	D'	C'	-

-   Playing each note, sing the song.
-   Practice several times until you can sing the song in consistent beat.

2. Play the song together in different ways.
   - Accompany the song.
     - Accompany the song by playing C and G on a xylophone while you sing the song.
     - One or more people can play the melody while others accompany by playing C and G.

   - At the end of the song, one improvises a melody.
     - While others accompany with C and G, one person plays improvised melody using C, D, E, G, and A.
     - Sing the song all together and at the end one person improvises for 8 beats.
     - Repeat it several times so that people can get a turn at improvising.

   - A pair of students can improvise.
     - After singing and playing the song, one student improvises 4 beats and the other student responds to it.
     - The second student can either repeat the melody (echoing) or make her/his own melody (question & answer improvisation).

3. Share your feeling and thoughts.
   - How did you feel?
     - Learning a new song
     - Playing on a xylophone
     - Playing together
     - Improvising melody
     - Improvising together
     - My feeling:

   - How did this activity change your thoughts? For example:
     - About playing a musical instrument
     - About improvisation
     - My thought:

   - How can you apply this activity to teach the children? For example:
     - The teacher can play the song and let the children improvise at the end of the song.
     - My idea:

7-3. Experiencing
7-3-(2) Playing for Music (Orff Method)

Activity 7-3-(2)

1. Playing voice
   - Using your voice, make rhythmical syllables (with no meaning) or a sentence.
   - The syllables can be as simple as "la la," "bum bum," or "'AE AE O, AE AE O."
   - The sentence can be any form. Some examples are "I am very happy," "Can you come and share the book?" and so forth.
   - What I made:

   - Repeat the syllables or the sentence so that you can be familiar with the pattern you made.

   - Organize the syllables (or sentences) in some way and perform in sequence.
   - The director can point to groups in random order.
   - Each group's verse can be repeated.
   - The director can signal any group in and out to add or subtract the sound.

2. Playing a non-pitched[1] musical instrument.
   - Think of different ways of using percussion instruments in class.
   - A simple activity or a game for motivation.
   - To use percussion instruments to support other activities such as storytelling
   - Other activities:

   - Make a pattern of rhythmical syllables or a sentence for each percussion instrument. For example:
   - "Chicka Chicka" (repeat 8 times) for maracas
   - "Tick-Tack, Tick-Tack, It Sounds Like a Ticking Clock" for a wood block.
   - More ideas:

   - Play in a group.
   - Each group can perform in sequence or in additive form, or in random order with a director's signal.
   - Speak the verbal phrase along with the instrument twice and then play instruments only.

---

[1] The percussion instruments which cannot make pitch. For example, drum, maraca, and so forth. An example of a pitched percussion instrument is a xylophone.

3. Research on music-teaching method related to playing musical instruments.
    - Research on the Orff Method.
    -   The Orff Method is a music-teaching method, developed by a German composer, Carl Orff (1895-1982).
    -   It is intended for groups of children singing and playing together.
    -   It emphasizes the development of creativity and the ability to improvise.
    -   Orff designed a special set of instruments such as xylophones, metalophones, and other percussion instruments.
    -   Other research:

    - Focus on Ostinato.
    -   It is an elemental structural device which persistently repeats a pattern or motive.[1]
    -   My research:

4. Talk about teaching children how to play musical instruments.

    - Share ideas on how to apply the Orff method to the curriculum. For example:
    -   Using Ostinato to memorize concepts of other subject areas.
    -   My idea:

    - Discuss issues in teaching how to play in a classroom setting. For example:
    -   Should the children learn how to play musical instruments in class?
    -   Is it necessary to teach how to read musical symbols in playing musical instruments?
    -   More issues:

---

[1] Saliba, K. (1996). *Austinato: An Ostinato Jamboree for Voices and Orff Instruments*. Lakeland, TN: Memphis Musicraft Publications

Reflection on Unit 7

1. At this juncture, what is your personal definition of:
   - Ostinato

2. What musical activities will you use in the classroom to:
   - Play musical instruments to accompany children's singing
   - Help children's playing

3. My reflection on the musical experience in Unit 7.
   - With respect to my personal learning and growth
   - In terms of my future teaching experience

When I dance, I move to the music.
When I play, I move with the music.

Unit 8: Creating Music

Improvisation
*

Musical work
Created spontaneously

.

We can create music
With no preparation

Composition
*

Musical work
Created precisely in advance

.

We can create music in a form
With preparation

Form
*

The shape of a musical composition

Unit 8
Creating Music

You will learn and reflect on music and teaching through:

8-1. Building Knowledge

8-1-(1) Creating Music
8-1-(2) Children's Creativity

8-2. Developing Skills

8-2-(1) Creating Music for Image
8-2-(2) Creating Music for Action

8-3. Experiencing

8-3-(1) Creating Music Together
8-3-(2) Creating for Music (MMCP Method)

8-1. Building Knowledge
8-1-(1) Creating Music

Activity 8-1-(1)

1. Learn about improvisation and composition
   - What are the similarities between improvisation and composition? For example:
   - Musical work
   - Creating Music
   - Way of music making
   - My thought:

   - What are the differences between improvisation and composition?
   - Improvisation needs no preparation while composition needs preparation.
   - Improvisation is creating music freely while composition is creating music in a form.
   - My thought:

2. Research and learn about the musical form.
   - Explain musical form. For example:
   - Musical form is the shape of a musical composition as defined by all of its pitches, rhythms, dynamics, and timbres.
   - The form shows how melodic/rhythmic patterns are organized in a musical piece.
   - There is a melodic pattern which can be a motive or a foundational idea to begin with. For example, in "Mary Had a Little Lamb," the first melodic part for the words "Mary had a little lamb" can be a motive A
   - We can repeat the motive and make another A, slightly change it and make A', make a new pattern B.

   - Analyze a children's song in terms of musical form. For example:
   - "Twinkle Twinkle Little Star": A (a-b)- B (b'-b')- A (a-b)
     a: Twinkle twinkle little star
     b: How I wonder what you are
     b': Up above the world so high

   - "London Bridge is Falling Down': A-B-A-C
     A: London bridge is falling down
     B: Falling down falling down
     A: London bridge is falling down
     C: My fair lady

   - My analysis:

- Make a different form of melodic pattern
    - Make a simple melodic pattern (A) on your xylophone in 8 measures.
    - Use the same melody for the first 4 measures and change the next 4 measures (A').
    - Make a new melodic pattern (B).
    - Use the same melodic pattern of B for the first 4 measures and change the next 4 measures (B').
    - My melodic pattern:

- Make a short musical piece in an organized form. For example:
    - A-A'-B-A',
    - A-B-B-A,
    - A-B-A-B,
    - A-A'-B-B',
    - A-B-A

8-1. Building Knowledge
8-1-(2) Children's Creativity

Activity 8-1-(2)

1. Research on creativity
   - Explain creativity or creative thinking.
   - Creative thinking is a process of thinking about elements in a new or unique way.[1]
   - Creative thinking involves divergent thinking to generate many possible solutions to a problem by expanding the number of alternatives.
   - Creativity is understood in individual talent, domain (discipline; area of which one's creativity is shown), and field (judges, institutions: judges of other people a creative person meets)[2]

2. Research on children's development of creativity.
   - How do children's musical characteristics of creative behavior occur? For example[3]:
   - Through the excitement generated by discovering, testing, and comparing instrumental sound
   - Creative singing often takes the form of chants, which occur extensively in spontaneous play activities
   - The key to developing innate musicality is improvisation.
   - My research:

   - How do teachers encourage children's musical creativity? For example:
   - Supportive physical and emotional environment, including musical instruments that produce beautiful sounds.[4]
   - Freedom of choice within structural limits
   - Children acquire the tools for creative compositions such as spontaneous songs or chant from the songs we teach them and the models teachers present.
   - Teachers can allow more time for creative tasks
   - Other thoughts:

---

[1] Sternberg, R. J. (1995). *In Search of the Human Mind.* New York: Harcourt Brace.
[2] Gardner, H. (1993). *Creating Minds.* NY: Basic Books, A Division of Harper Collins Publishers, Inc.
[3] Moorhead, G. E., & Pond, D. (1978). *Music of Young Children.* Santa Barbara, CA: Pillsbury Foundation for Advancement of Music Education.
[4] Shelley, S. (1981). Investigating the Musical Capabilities of Young Children. *Council for Research in Music Education, 68,* 26-34

8-2. Developing Skills
8-2-(1) Creating Music for Image

Activity 8-2-(1)

1. Musical poem
    -   Create a poem.
    -   Poem with 4 lines might be good.
    -   You can use repeated syllables in each line, like a rhyme.
    -   Make each line the same in length.
    -   The poem I wrote:

    -   Make a rhythm or melody for the poem you created.
    -   Make a rhythmic or melodic pattern for the first line.
    -   You can use the same pattern for the next line.
    -   As described in 8-1-1, you can use musical form such as ABBA.
    -   My idea:

2. Musical drawing
    -   Search for the pictures or drawings with which you might be able to create music. For example:
    -   Pictures with different lines
    -   Pictures with color contrast
    -   Pictures with images such as nature
    -   My search:

    -   Improvise music with musical instruments to express one of the pictures you selected:
    -   Lines in a drawing can be played in different melody
    -   Shape can give you an idea of how to play musical instruments
    -   My improvisation:

    -   Create your own pictures you might be using for children's music creating.
    -   My drawing:

8-2. Developing Skills
8-2-(2) Creating Music for Action

Activity 8-2-(2)

1. You can create music for action or movement.
   - Research children's books or video tapes with action to be played with musical instruments.
   - Books about cars, animals, people working, and so forth
   - Movies with musical action such as "Wildlife animals"[1]
   - My search:

   - Discuss how each action can be expressed with music.
   - What kind of musical instruments can express a certain action best?
   - How should we play musical instruments to play a certain action?
   - My idea:

2. You can create music for a story.
   - Research children's books to be used for music making. For example:
   - Books with short and simple words
   - Books with imitating words
   - Books with Expressive words
   - My search:

   - Using one of the books, practice how you can improvise music with musical instruments. For example, you can play musical instruments:
   - Whenever you read a certain word or a sentence.
   - Right after you read a certain word or a sentence.
   - Instead of reading a certain word or a sentence.

   - Discuss how you can apply the activity for children.
   - We can make a game such as: 1) each group picks a card, 2) Each card shows which page or part of the storybook the group will play, 3) Each group decides how they will play while the story is read.
   - You or the children can make up stories to be played.
   - My idea:

---

[1] Reader's Digeset. (1993). *Wildlife Symphony*. CA: The Reader's Digest Association , Inc.

8-3. Experiencing
8-3-(1) Creating Music Together

Activity 8-3-(1)

1. Create music together in a group.
   - Make a decision on what kind of music your group will create. For example:
   - A song
   - Music for dancing
   - Music for a movie clip
   - What our group made:

   - Create music.
   - Make a motive and develop it to a form.
   - Decided which instrument each member will play for each part.
   - Make a decision on another aspect of music such as tempo and dynamics (where to play fast/slow and loud/quiet).
   - Practice several times
   - My group's music:

2. Share music together
   - Each group performs the music.
   - If the music was made for a song, dance, or so forth, perform with it.
   - Record each group's performance

   - Share your thoughts and/or feeling on creating music. For example:
   - In the process of making music
   - In the process of practicing
   - In the process of performing
   - In the process of listening to others' music
   - My thoughts and feeling:

3. How can you share this experience with the children?

8-3. Experiencing
8-3-(2) Creating for Music (MMCP Method)

Activity 8-3-(2)

1. Research music-teaching methods focusing on creating music.
    *   Research MMCP method[1]. For example:
    -   The MMCP Interaction is a comprehensive early childhood music learning plan produced by the Manhattanville Music Curriculum Program, developed as a basic experience in musicianship for children of the preprimary and primary grades.
    -   The nature of it necessitates and indeed tends to create an atmosphere which is non-inhibiting.
    -   It deals with five objective areas: 1) experience within the creative process itself; 2) development of sensitivity to sounds, their interaction and musical nature; 3) understanding of basic concepts of musical elements, their combination and manipulation; 4) acquisition of the simple skills which allow the child to operate as a creative musician; and 5) development of positive attitudes toward music and self.

    *   Focus on how the MMCP method encourages children's creativity through musical exploration. For example:
    -   Phase I- Free exploration: To encourage the manipulation of a wide range of sound-producing materials, since every child is capable of creative activity and has the desire to engage in such activity.
    -   Phase II-Guided exploration: Encourages children to investigate their sound sources in greater depth, with guidance in finding new sounds which are necessary to sustain enthusiasm and involvement, and extension of free exploration.
    -   Phase III- Exploratory improvisation: the extensive creative interaction of children with one another and with numerous sounds, discovering new relationships of sounds and structuring a variety of expressive combinations and patterns.
    -   Phase IV- Planned improvisation: children organize their newly discovered patterns and combinations of sounds into compositions which are expressive and aesthetically satisfying to them.
    -   Phase V-Reapplication: Children learn that they can manipulate and organize the materials of music in ways that infer many different moods and feelings.

---

[1] Biasini, A., & Pogonowski, L. *MMCP Interaction: Early Childhood Music Curriculum.* Second Edition. WA: Americole

2. Share your thoughts and feeling on creativity.
   - Share your thoughts on what classroom teachers can do to encourage children's creativity through musical exploration in each phase. For example:
   - For phase I, provide a wide range of sound-producing materials so that children can explore freely.
   - For phase II, develop questions we might be able to ask children to encourage them to investigate a way to make sound in depth.
   - For phase III, interact with children in a creative way and encourage them to interact with other children to create a variety of expressive sound combinations and patterns.
   - For Phase IV, find ways to help children organize music they have created.
   - For Phase V, plan activities for different times when children can apply their music-creating process.
   - My idea:

   - How do you feel about creativity? For example:
   - Do you think you are creative? Why?
   - Does it affect your efficacy in teaching children for their creativity?
   - How can you help yourself to be creative?
   - My feeling and thought:

Reflection on Unit 8

1. At this juncture, what is your personal definition of:
   - Improvisation
   - Composition
   - Musical form

2. What musical activities will you use in the classroom to:
   - Create music to express poems or visual images
   - Create music for action or movement

3. My reflection on the musical experience in Unit 8.
   - With respect to my personal learning and growth
   - In terms of my future teaching experience

One may not have an ability to create a new thing,
but anyone can be creative in using things.

Unit 9: Music and an Integrated Curriculum

Curriculum
*

Learning Experience

.

It occurs in an educational setting

.

It is planned or unplanned

Integrated Curriculum
*

Synthesize information and
transfer knowledge across discipline areas

.

Helps students make valuable connections
during learning experiences

.

Helps children more to effectively
solve real-world problems

Unit 9

Music and an Integrated Curriculum

You will learn and reflect on music and teaching through:

9-1. Building Knowledge

9-1-(1) Music and a Curriculum
9-1-(2) Music and an Integrated Curriculum

9-2. Developing Skills

9-2-(1) Designing a Curriculum Model
9-2-(2) Ways to Integrate Music

9-3. Experiencing

9-3-(1) Music in Education
9-3-(2) Music and Teachers

9-1. Building Knowledge
9-1-(1) Music and Curriculum

Activity 9-1-(1)

1. Learn about a curriculum.
   - Search how a curriculum has been defined in a traditional curriculum history. For example[1]:
   - The cumulative tradition of organized knowledge
   - An instructional plan or course of study
   - Measured instructional outcomes (products)
   - Cultural reproduction

   - Search how curriculum has been defined by progressives. For example:
   - Knowledge selection/organization from the experience of a culture
   - Modes of thought
   - Experience

   - Define curriculum in your own words. For example:
   - Curriculum is learning experience students get in an educational setting.
   - My definition:

2. Discuss the relationship between music and the curriculum.
   - Discuss how music can be viewed depending on how you see a curriculum. For example:
   - (From a traditional view...) music can be viewed as a part of knowledge and teachers teach musical concepts.
   - If the curriculum is viewed as an instructional plan, music could be considered as doing music activities, and music curriculum as planning music activities.
   - Music can be included in all learning experiences that have music components.
   - My thought:

   - Share your position on how we should view music and curriculum.

---

[1] Tanner, D. & Tanner, L. N. (1995). *Curriculum Development: Theory into Practice*. Ch. 5. Changing Conceptions of Curriculum NJ: Prentice-Hall. Inc.

9-1. Building Knowledge
9-1-(2) Music and an Integrated Curriculum

Activity 9-1-(2)

---

1. Learn about integrated curriculum.
   - Search for the definition. For example[1]:
   - It is a curriculum to integrate information and develop a set of clearly defined links between themes, topics, and discipline areas.
   - My definition:

2. Discuss issues related to an integrated curriculum.
   - What are the advantages of an integrated curriculum? For example:
   - It assists students in synthesizing information and transfering knowledge across discipline areas in order to help them better solve real-world problems.[2]
   - My thought:

   - What are the limitations of an integrated curriculum? For example[3]:
   - To integrate subjects can promote progress toward significant goals in one subject but not in another because it links theme-related contents of each subject area.
   - Ill-conceived integration ideas sometimes require students to do inappropriate activities. For example, the children may be asked to sing a certain song because it contains the words related to a theme, but it may not be appropriate at children's developmental level.
   - My thought:

   - From this discussion on curriculum, what suggestions can we draw in integrating music into a curriculum?

---

[1] Nielsen, M. E. (1989). Integrative Learning for Young Children: A Thematic Approach. *Educational Horizons*, 68(1), 19-24.
[2] Nielsen, M. E. (1989). Integrative Learning for Young Children: A thematic Approach. *Educational Horizons*, 68(1), 19-24.
[3] Brophy, J., & Alleman, J. (1991). A Caveat: Curriculum Integration Isn't Always a Good Idea. *Educational Leadership*, 49(2).66-64.

9-2. Developing Skills
9-2-(1) Designing a Curriculum Model

Activity 9-2-(1)

---

1. Curriculum Sources
   - Describe the sources that influence curriculum. For example[1]:
   - <u>Society</u>: contemporary life needs, social demands, etc.
   - <u>Knowledge</u>: subject matter, curriculum, behavioral science, etc.
   - <u>Learner</u>: developmental needs, group dynamics, etc.

   - Describe the elements we should consider in designing a curriculum. For example:
   - <u>Objectives</u>: Aim, Educational goal, Instructional objectives
   - <u>Methods</u>: Teaching strategies, approaches, activities
   - <u>Assessment</u>
   - Other elements to consider:

   - When teaching music, how can we consider the sources and/or elements of curriculum? For example:
   - <u>Society</u>: We can use different societal music sources such as concerts, music libraries, etc.
   - My thought:

2. Curriculum Design Model
   - Draw a map to follow when you design a curriculum. For instance:
   - Draw spaces for curriculum sources such as society, knowledge, and learner.
   - Draw spaces for curriculum elements such as objectives, methods, and assessment.
   - Connect sources and elements using lines, arrows, and so forth.
   - Elements don't have to be in the same row, or in consecutive order.
   - My Model:

   - Share your model
   - Explain it, by using an example of how the model is associated in music teaching.
   - Share the limitations of your model.
   - My thought:

---

[1] Tanner, D., & Tanner, L. N. (1995). *Curriculum Development: Theory into Practice*. Ch. 8. Sources and forces for curriculum renewal-society, knowledge, and the learner. NJ: Prentice-Hall, Inc.

9-2. Developing Skills
9-2-(2) Ways to Integrate Music

Activity 9-2-(2)

---

1. Research different ways to integrate curriculum.
   - Research different models to integrate. For example[1]:
   - <u>Nested Model</u>: Within each subject area, the teacher targets multiple skills such as social skill, a thinking skill, and a content-specific skill.
   - <u>Webbed Model</u>: fertile theme is webbed to curriculum contents and disciplines.
   - <u>Threaded Model</u>: threads thinking skills, social skills, multiple intelligences, technology, and study skills through the various disciplines.
   - My search:

   - Apply each model into your curriculum planning to see how it works for music. For example:
   - <u>Music in a nested model</u>: To teach music, a teacher might develop ways to let children work together, questions to encourage children's thinking skills, and hands-on activity to learn certain musical concepts.
   - My application:

2. Design a curriculum.
   - Using the webbed model, design an integrated curriculum[2]
   - Select a conceptual theme to be placed at the hub of a thematic web and develop a main idea.
   - Select sub-unit topics and main ideas to identify several thematically related topics.
   - Join the central concept/theme to the carious sub-unit topics through clarifying phrases or statements.
   - Divide each topical sub-unit into specific discipline
   - Outline activities within sub-units
   - My design:

---

[1] Fogarty, R. (1991). Ten Ways to Integrate Curriculum. *Educational Leadership*, 49(2), 61-65.
[2] Nielsen, M. E. (1989). Integrative Learning for Young Children: A Thematic Approach. *Educational Horizons*, 68(1), 19-24.

9-3. Experiencing
9-3-(1) Music in Education

Activity 9-3-(1)

1. Research music in an educational context.
   - Review some of the popular early childhood educational programs and their main ideas. For example:
     - F. Froebel's Kindergarten (19th century): Education through gift and occupation
     - M. Montessori's "Casa dei Bambini (children's house)"[1]: Practical life/Prepared environment- sensory materials, academic materials for writing, reading and mathematics.
     - High/Scope[2]: Knowledge construction through active participation of children/ Regular daily planning by the teaching staff/ Developmentally sequenced goals
     - My search:

   - Search how music has been used in early childhood education. For example:
     - Froebelian[3]: Music has had a prominent role. Froebel had established children's songs as an important instructional medium.
     - Montessorian [4]: Like other activities, music is taught through self-directed activities in a prepared environment.
     - My search:

2. Share thoughts on music in education
   - How has music been used in different educational programs?

   - How do you feel about using music in an educational context? For example:
     - Using different music teaching approaches for different programs such as Montessori or High/scope program.
     - Finding appropriate music selections or activities for a program
     - My feeling:

---

[1] Montessori, M. (1967). *The Montessori Method* (A.E. George, Trans.) Cambridge, MA: Bentley
[2] High/Scope Education Resesarch Foundation (1989). *The High/Scope K-3 Curriculum: An Introduction*, Ypsilanti, MI
[3] Froebel, F. (1904). *Pedagogies of the Kindergarten* (J. Jarvis, Trans.). New York: D. Appletoon & Co.
[4] Montessori, M. (1964). *The Advanced Montessori Method: The Montessori Elementary Materials.* Cambridge, MA: Robert Bentley.

9-3. Experiencing
9-3-(2) Music and Teachers

Activity 9-3-(2)

---

1. Share your thoughts and feeling in teaching music.
    - How do you feel about teaching music? For example:
    - Teaching musical concepts such as timbre, rhythm, melody, and so forth.
    - Using musical skills such as singing, playing, and so forth.
    - Integrating music into a whole curriculum.
    - My Feeling:

    - How do you think you can improve your teaching skills?

2. Share your thoughts and feeling on having the position of music teacher.
    - What are the advantages of having a music teacher in early childhood or elementary class? For example:
    - Children can get musical knowledge in depth.
    - Classroom teachers get less burdened in teaching music.
    - My thought:

    - What are some limitations of having a music teacher in early childhood or elementary class?
    - Children may not get enough musical support in class.
    - Music may not be integrated well because it is taught separately.
    - My thought:

    - How can we improve music teaching in an early childhood or elementary classroom? For example:
    - Appropriate teacher education considering teachers' needs.
    - Communication and cooperation of music teacher and classroom teacher
    - My thought:

Reflection on Unit 9

1. At this juncture, what is your personal definition of:
   - Curriculum
   - Integrated curriculum

2. What musical activities will you use in the classroom to:
   - Integrate music into other curriculum areas
   - Reflect sources and elements of curriculum

3. My reflection on the musical experience in Unit 9.
   - With respect to my personal learning and growth
   - In terms of my future teaching experience

*As we see a map to find a location of the spot we are looking for,
we need to see a map called "curriculum" to see where music is in education.*

Unit 10: Music and the Environment

Environment
*

A setting of relations one experiences
Conscious, or unconsciously

.

Plays a key role in children's behavior

Unit 10
Music and the Environment

You will learn and reflect on music and teaching through:

10-1. Building Knowledge

10-1-(1) Music and Environment
10-1-(2) Children and Environment

10-2. Developing Skills

10-2-(1) Physical Environment
10-2-(2) Social Environment

10-3. Experiencing

10-3-(1) Environmental Music
10-3-(2) Teachers for Musical Environment

10-1. Building Knowledge
10-1-(1) Musical Environment

Activity 10-1-(1)

1. Learn about environment.
   - What is an environment? For example:
   - Physical or social surrounding: Physical environment (such as manipulative materials or visual aids) and social environment (such as interaction between a child and other children or a teacher)
   - Systems of relations that a child experiences[1]: 1) Microsystems such as play area, family, schools, or peers, 2) mesosystems made up of the interrelations among two or more settings, 3) exosystems such as extended family, friends of family, or mass media, 4) macrosystems such as attitudes and ideologies of the culture, and 5) chronosystems such as time.
   - My search and thought:

   - What are guidelines for a classroom arrangement to support children's development? For example[2]:
   - Open areas: you and your children can meet as a whole group
   - Center areas: well-defined and accessible to children with appropriate and abundant materials for children's use
   - All kinds of activities (in center areas): quiet areas such as reading and puzzle, and loud areas such as woodworking and blocks
   - Materials: children can easily retrieve, easily store.
   - My search:

2. Think about a classroom setting as an environment.
   - Draw a floor map of a classroom setting. For example:
   - Draw a layout of learning centers
   - Describe basic materials provided in each area
   - My floor map:

   - Check if the floor map is appropriate. For example:
   - Locate quiet areas together and loud areas together
   - Have large space for a whole group activity and a unit for individual activity.
   - Space with table and chairs or rug needed.
   - My check:

---

[1] Bronfenbrenner, U. (1979). *The Ecology of Human Development: Experiments by Nature and Design.* Cambridge: Harvard University Press.
[2] Morrison, G. S. (2001). *Early Childhood Education Today.* 8th Edition. NJ: Merrill Prentice Hall

3. Think about a musical environment
   - Explain how a classroom setting can incorporate a musical environment. For example:
     - Materials to encourage children's musical development in each area
     - Musical concepts related to materials or children's play in each area.
     - How Musical or music-related interaction can be occurred in class
     - My thought:

   - Think about what kind of environment will be needed for children's musical development. For example:
     - Space to listen, to sing, to move expressively and rhythmically, to play, and to create.
     - Space large enough for music activities such as group singing or movement and a tangible unit where children can interact with one another.
     - My thought:

   - Discuss what we should consider for music in a large group. For example:
     - Space is large enough so that children don't bump each other while interacting.
     - Do not block the pathways to other learning areas.
     - My thought:

   - Discuss what we should consider for music in learning centers for individual learning. For example:
     - Reflect children's individual interests
     - Materials provided to explore musical instruments, listen to music, and so forth.
     - Consider children's development
     - My thought:

10-1. Building Knowledge
10-1-(2) Children and Environment

Activity 10-1-(2)

1. Learn about theories of children's development and learning.
   - Why is it important to understand children's development? For example:
   - It helps to understand children's behavior.
   - It helps to provide an appropriate environment for children's learning
   - My thought:

   - What are children's development theories? For example[1]:
   - Maturational theory: Particular behaviors emerge at predetermined times, depending on the individual's inherited biological timetable, and that the timing is unaffected by environment or experience
   - Psychoanalytic theory: Behavior is a function of interaction of the id, seeking gratification; the superego, setting limits; and the ego, directing the id to find satisfaction in acceptable ways.
   - Learning theory: Behavior is influenced by an environment such as stimulus, reward, and reinforcement.
   - Cognitive-Developmental Theory (Jean Piaget): Children construct knowledge gradually through interaction with the environment
   - The Sociocultural theory (Lev Vygotsky): a child internalizes knowledge as a result of dialectic interaction with more mature members of his or her culture.
   - More research on each theory:

   - What are the differences between developmental theories? For example:
   - Maturational theory views children's nature as a major component of development while learning theory views environmental effects as an important factor
   - Cognitive-Developmental theory sees children's physical interaction as a major source of constructing knowledge, while the sociocultural theory has social interaction as an important part.
   - My thoughts:

---

[1] Schickedanz, J. A., Schickendaz, D. I., Forshth, P. D., & Forsyth, G. A. (2001). Ch. 1 Theories of Child Development and Methods of Studying Children. Pp. 38-39. *In Understanding Children and Adolescents*. 4th Edition. Boston: Allyn and Bacon.

2. Discuss how to apply theories of children's development in providing musical environment.

    - How can we apply each theory of children's development into music teaching and learning? For example:

    -   Maturational theory: Since children's particular behaviors emerge at predetermined times, it's important to know children's inherited biological timetable. Based on children's determined music behavior such as singing in certain ranges, we should plan music activities to be appropriate for children's development.

    -   Psychoanalytic theory: Music can provide ways to satisfy children's gratification by helping them express their feeling through rhythmic movement, playing instruments, or singing.

    -   Learning theory: Children's musical behavior can be influenced by an environment teachers provide. For instance, a teacher can give a stimulus, reward, or reinforcement for children's musical behavior, or use music as an environment for behavior in other areas.

    -   Cognitive-Developmental Theory (Jean Piaget): It's important to provide musical environment so that children can construct their musical knowledge through interaction

    -   The Sociocultural theory (Lev Vygotsky): Teachers' or more competent peers' interaction with a child is very important because a child constructs knowledge through it.

    -   More thoughts:

    - Discuss how you would deal with issues related children's musical behavior when theories conflict with each other. For example:

    -   Should we sing songs only in children's vocal range?

    -   Should the teacher intervene when a child interacts with musical instrument in music area?

    -   Should we play happy or sad music for children in a certain mood?

    -   Other issues and thoughts:

10-2. Developing Skills
10-2-(1) Physical Environment

Activity 10-2-(1)

1. Design a music area in the classroom setting.
   - What should we consider in setting up a music area? For example:
   - Noise level: where to locate
   - Space: how many children can play in the area
   - Materials: Listening, reading, and playing materials.
   - Other ideas:

   - What are the limitations of setting up a music area in a classroom? For example:
   - We cannot control the volume of certain musical instruments.
   - Not enough music materials
   - My thought:

   - Design a music area and discuss the advantages and limitations of your model. For example:
   - Does it provide children space for listening, playing, singing, and moving?
   - Does it help children's musical knowledge, skills, and dispositions?
   - Does it encourage children's musical interaction with other children as well as materials?
   - My discussion:

2. Make musical instruments
   - Think of the ways to make musical instruments?
   - Review Unit 1 and think of musical instruments you can make using recycled materials.
   - Think of the instruments children can make as classroom activities.
   - My idea:

   - Set up a table to make musical instruments in an art area.
   - Bring materials needed for a certain instrument.
   - Set up materials so that children can use them at easy access (e.g., Funnels to put grains or rice into a bottle)
   - Provide materials to decorate instruments.
   - Tools to dry and/or clean up

3. Make musical materials
   - Make musical materials for children's use. For example:
   - Listening tape with picture cards to be provided in music corner
   - Picture book about music
   - Other ideas:

   - Make musical materials for teaching. For example:
   - Visual aids to be used in teaching new songs.
   - Flash cards for a simple rhythmic game to be used for a transition activity.
   - Music pictures to be hung on the wall.
   - My idea:

10-2. Developing Skills
10-2-(2) Social Environment

Activity 10-2-(2)

1. Discuss instruction in a social environment for children's learning.
    - What can be done in a social environment that you can consider in a curriculum for children's learning? For example:
    - Interaction between a teacher and children, a child with other children.
    - Ways of instruction such as verbal instruction, modeling, and reinforcement.
    - Environment where children experience different cultures
    - Other thoughts:

    - What are ways of instruction to help children's learning? For example:
    - Verbal instruction such as dispositional praise or positive attribution
    - Observational learning through modeling
    - Reinforcement such as positive reinforcement; something that is added to the environment after the person acts. For example, a reward can encourage the person to maintain the action.
    - My thoughts:

2. Develop ways of instruction as a social environment to help children's musical learning.
    - How can verbal instruction help children's musical learning? For example:
    - Children can respond to dispositional praise such as "you are a good listener" when a teacher communicates after children's music listening.
    - A teacher can give suggestions while a child tries to make music or play musical instruments.
    - A teacher can ask open-ended questions for children's musical creativity.
    - My idea:

    - How can you model musical behavior to help children's musical learning? For example:
    - Respond to background music by rhythmic movement.
    - Chant musically in communicating with children.
    - My idea:

    - How can you use reinforcement to help children's musical learning? For example:
    - Respond to children's behavior using musical or instrumental sound; play a bell for good behavior.
    - Other ideas:

10-3. Experiencing
10-3-(1) Environmental Music

Activity 10-3-(1)

1. Share your feeling and thoughts about background music.
   - When do you play music as a background? For example:
   - Studying
   - Driving
   - I listen to music when:

   - How does background music affect your activity? For example:
   - It can help the activity by changing mood
   - It can distract while studying
   - My feeling:

2. Organize a personal music library.
   - Make a list of music you have.

   - Share why you bought the CD and how you feel when you listen to the music. For example:
   - You may like a song because it is soothing
   - You might have bought it because you liked a singer's voice.
   - A movie sound track might help remind you of the movie.
   - What I have and why:

   - Organize the music CD's you have so that you can use them for your teaching. For example:
   - By musical concepts such as timbre, rhythm, harmony, and so forth
   - By theme such as animal, nature, etc.
   - My music:

   - If you are collecting more for your music library, what would you need to help your teaching? For example:
   - Music from different cultures
   - What I would collect and why

10-3. Experiencing
10-3-(2) Teachers for Musical Environment

Activity 10-3-(2)

1. Share your thoughts about teachers' qualities for music environment
   - What are attributes of teachers who create a musical environment? For example[1]:
     - Willing to invest time and effort in getting to know children's musical development, interest, needs, and/or desires.
     - Model musical behaviors
     - Have a sense of humor, smile, laugh, play with, and enjoy the children.
     - Plan musical experiences reflecting children's interest
     - Provide children time and opportunity for musical experiences
     - Realize children's own rates and unique ways of learning and provide process-oriented learning
     - Evaluate music by planning, lessons, and so forth.
     - My thought:

2. Share your feelings on your musical qualities.
   - What do you think are the musical qualities you have?

   - What are the qualities in which you have no confidence?

---

[1] Adopted from... McDonald, D. T., & Simons, G. M. (1989). *Musical Growth and Development: Birth Through Six*. Ch. 4: Planning the Environment. *P*.75. NY: Schirmer Books, A Division of Macmillan, Inc.

Reflection on Unit 10

1. At this juncture, what is your personal definition of:
   • Environment

2. What activities will you do in the classroom to:
   • Design a music area in a classroom setting
   • Make musical instruments and/or musical materials
   • Develop musical interaction to help children's musical learning

3. My reflection on the musical experience in Unit 10.
   • With respect to my personal learning and growth
   • In terms of my future teaching experience

*We cannot but experience music
because we live in music.*

Unit 11: Music and Practice

Standards
*

What students should acquire
And be able to do

.

In understanding knowledge
Developing skills
Appreciating music

Theory
*

A set of systematically organized assumptions

.

It helps to understand children's behavior
To plan a musical activity

Unit 11
Music and Practice

You will learn and reflect on music and teaching through:

11-1. Building Knowledge

11-1-(1) Music and Standards
11-1-(2) Music and Developmental Theory

11-2. Developing Skills

11-2-(1) Planning Music
11-2-(2) Daily Music

11-3. Experiencing

11-3-(1) Teaching Music
11-3-(2) Developmentally Appropriate Practice

11-1. Building Knowledge
11-1-(1) Music and Standards

1. Learn about standards.
    - What are they and why are they important? For example[1]:
    - To think of what students should know and be able to do
    - They help define what a good education should provide thorough grounding in a basic body of knowledge and the skills required both to make sense and make use of the discipline.
    - Adopting standards, schools are taking a stand for rigor in the area of education that has too often, and wrongly, been treated as optional.
    - My thought:

    - What kind of standards or statements can we refer to for teaching music in class? For example:
    - National Standards for Music Education, developed by MENC (The National Association for Music Education)
    - INTASC (Interstate New Teacher Assessment And Support Consortium) Standards for Arts Education, developed by CCSSO (Council of Chief State School Officers)[2]
    - State Learning Standards such as New York State Learning Standards for the Arts, developed by NYSSMA (The New York State School Music Association)[3]
    - NAEYC Position Statements: developed by NAEYC (National Association for the Education of Young Children) to improve program practice with children, policies affecting early childhood programs, and early childhood professional development and professionalism
    - The standard of excellence in teacher preparation: provided by NCATE (The National Council for Accreditation of Teacher Education)[4].
    - My search:

---

[1] http://www.menc.org/publication/books/summary.html

[2] http://www.ccsso.org/projects/Interstate_New_Teacher_Assessment_and_Support_Consortium/Projects/Standards_Development/

[3] http://www.nysatl.nysed.gov/standards.html

[4] http://www.ncate.org/standard/m_stds.htm

2. Research and summarize music and teaching-related standards classroom teachers might be able to refer to.
    - INTASC Core Principles[1]
    - <u>Principle 1</u>: Subject matter knowledge-To understand music in its process (how), purposes and functions (why), contexts (when/where), roles (who), and product (what).
    - <u>Principle 2</u>: Child development-To design and implement developmentally appropriate music instruction to support children's development in music
    - <u>Principle 3</u>: Diversity of learners-To understand and use different learning styles and culture in teaching music
    - <u>Principle 4</u>: Instructional strategies-To help children develop creative and critical thinking skills in and through music.
    - <u>Principle 5</u>: Learning environment-To create positive learning environment for music
    - <u>Principle 6</u>: Communication-To observe, listen, and communicate with children in ways that encourage continued exploration in music.
    - <u>Principle 7</u>: Planning/Integrated instruction- To plan an instruction based upon knowledge of music, students, the community, and curriculum goals.
    - <u>Principle 8</u>: Assessment-To understand informal and formal types of assessment for music
    - <u>Principle 9</u>: Self-reflection/Professional development-To gauge own professional development through music and seek feedback to improve teaching of music.
    - <u>Principle 10</u>: Community involvement-To recognize music as an integral part of larger community and to get a variety of resources to enrich and support music programs from the community.

    - National Standards for Music Education[2]
    - Singing, alone and with others, a varied repertoire of music.
    - Performing on instruments, alone and with others, a varied repertoire of music.
    - Improvising melodies, variations, and accompaniments.
    - Composing and arranging music within specified guidelines.
    - Reading and notating music.
    - Listening to, analyzing, and describing music.
    - Evaluating music and music performances.
    - Understanding relationships between music, the other arts, and disciplines outside the arts.
    - Understanding music in relation to history and culture.

---

[1] http://www.ccsso.org/content/pdfs/ArtsStandards.pdf
[2] http://www.menc.org/publication/books/standards.htm

- Learning Standards for the Arts[1]:
  - Standard 1: Creating, performing, and participating in the arts- Students will actively engage in the processes that constitute creation and performance in the arts (dance, music, theatre, and visual arts) and participate in various roles in the arts
  - Standard 2: Knowing and using arts materials and resources- Students will be knowledgeable about and make use of the materials and resources available for participation in the arts in various arts
  - Standard 3: Responding to and analyzing works of art- Students will respond critically to a variety of works in the arts, connecting the individual work to other works and to other aspects of human endeavor and thought.
  - Standard 4: Understanding the cultural dimensions and contributions of the arts- Students will develop an understanding of the personal and cultural forces that shape artistic communication and how the arts in turn shape the diverse cultures of past and present society

- NAEYC Standards for Early Childhood Professional Preparation[2]:
  - Standard 1: Promoting Child Development and Learning
  - Standard 2: Building Family and Community Relationship
  - Standard 3: Observing, Documenting, and Assessing to Support Young Children and Families
  - Standard 4: Teaching and Learning;
    4a) Connecting with children and families
    4b) Using developmentally effective approaches
    4c) Understanding content knowledge in early education
    4d) Building meaningful curriculum
  - Standard 5: Becoming a professional

- Organize music standards in your own way so that you can reflect those in learning activities you plan for children. For example:

Instructional Objectives	Standards	Methods Activities	Assessment
(What my students will achieve)	(Standards of what my objectives demonstrate)	(How I will teach)	(How I will know whether the objectives are accomplished)

---

[1] Standards-based instructional model, developed by The New York State School Music Association (NYSSMA)

[2] http://www.naeyc.org/profdev/prep_review/2001.pdf

11-1. Building Knowledge
11-1-(2) Music Instruction and Children's Learning

Activity 11-1-(2)

1. Discuss the relationship between children's learning and music teaching and/or instruction.
   - What are different ways of providing music instruction?
   - Providing musical environment to encourage children's musical interaction
   - Personal or instrumental stimulation through modeling or accompanying
   - Different tasks in music activities such as singing with words or humming
   - My thoughts:

   - What can be the effect of music instruction? For example:
   - Certain types of instruction can promote children's musical development
   - The same instruction can affect children in different ways because of children's individuality
   - The same musical concepts can be delivered in different ways and levels, depending on the instruction.
   - My thought:

2. Review research studies about how musical instruction affects children's development.
   - What does research say about musical environment?
   - Children who are exposed to a richer musical environment show a greater and earlier ability to carry a melody than those children whose musical environments are poorer[1]

   - What does research say about music instruction for children's ability in pitch, melody, and harmony?
   - Children were more easily able to match a pitch presented by a female rather than a male voice[2]
   - Children sing better with melodic replication or traditional tonal harmonic accompaniment than with either chromatic or dissonant harmonic accompaniment[3]

---

[1] Drexler, E. N. (1938). A Study of the Development of the Ability to Carry a Melody at the Preschool Level. *Child Development*, 9(2), 319-322.
[2] Green, G. A. (1989). The Effect of Vocal Modeling on Pitch-Matching Accuracy of Elementary School Children. *Journal of Research in Music Education*, 38(3), 226-231
[3] Stauffer, S. L. (1985). *An Investigation of the Effects of Melodic and Harmonic Context on Development of Singing Ability in Primary Grade Children.* Dissertation Abstract International, 46, 1862A.

3. How can you apply research results in educational practice?
    - Discuss whether research on children's development or instructional methods implies certain practice. For example:
        - Children prefer music with fast tempo in listening and playing.[1] Should we use more fast music than slow music?
        - Instrumental and noninstrumental treatment groups did not differ significantly in perception of the melodic components.[2] Does this mean it does not matter whether we use musical instruments in music activities?
        - Color-coded materials had a positive influence in that children favored the color-coded notation as easier to play, but it did not affect children's sight-read or memory tasks.[3] Are color-coded materials effective?
        - My thought:

    - While discussing, write down practical issues you might want to reflect on. For example:
        - Children's preference and what's educational.
        - How children respond and their actual development.
        - My thought:

---

[1] LeBlanc, A., & Cote, R. (1983). Effects of Tempo and Performing Medium on Children's Music Preference. *Journal of Research in Music Education*, v31, n 1, pp 57-66

[2] Ramsey, J. H. (1983). The Effects of Age, Singing Ability, and Instrumental Experiences on Preschool Children's Melodic Perception. *Journal of Research in Music Education*, v 31, n.2, pp 133-145

[3] Rogers, G. L. (1991). Effects of Color-Coded Notation on Music Achievement of Elementary Instrumental Students. *Journal of Research in Music Education*, v.39, n.1, pp.64-73.

11-2. Developing Skills
11-2-(1) Planning Music

Activity 11-2-(1)

---

1. Learn about lesson planning.
    *   What is it?
    -   Teaching guidelines
    -   My definition:

    *   State elements to be included in a lesson plan. For example:
    -   Whom to teach: Consider child development.
    -   When to teach: Time distribution and teaching context.
    -   What to teach: Theme, topics, and so forth.
    -   Why teach: Rationale such as aim, educational goal, or instructional objectives.
    -   How to teach: Materials, Procedures including motivational activity and culmination, and Assessment.

2. Learn about elements of a lesson plan
    *   Discuss what to consider for students you teach.
    -   Their developmental level?
    -   Individual difference such as diversity of learning styles.

    *   Discuss what is to be considered for time. For example:
    -   When we will have music time in daily schedule.
    -   How long musical activity will be.
    -   How to distribute time for each part of lesson.

    *   Discuss what to consider for a theme.
    -   It can be a musical concept such as pitch or rhythm.
    -   It can be a topic from a thematic unit such as animals or transportation.
    -   It can be a more abstract theme to cover a broader area such as change.

    *   Discuss what are aim and instructional objectives.
    -   The aim is a brief sentence or a question to give a general idea about the lesson.
    -   Instructional objectives are what children will achieve by the end of the lesson.
    -   Objectives can be described in cognitive, behavioral, and affective domains.
        a. Cognitive objective states concepts or knowledge children will learn.
        b. Behavioral objective states skills children will develop.
        c. Affective objective states attitude children will gain.

152 **[Unit 11]**
    The Musical Teacher:
    Preparing Teacher to Use Music in the Childhood Classroom

- Share ideas on what should be considered for materials in music.
  - Teaching aids such as visual materials, CDs, books, videos, computers, etc.
  - Materials to be provided for children to use
  - Musical instruments to play

- Discuss what is to be considered for procedure.
  - You can begin with a motivational activity that is a simple activity or a game to be focused on or relative to the main activity.
  - The procedure should be well organized and practical to be reliable.
  - It should reflect objectives.
  - Questions you might ask in the procedure can be included under each step.
  - You might need more ideas (for other possibilities) written even though you might not need to use all of them in an actual lesson.

- Share your thoughts on assessment. For example:
  - It's the way to check whether instructional objectives are achieved.
  - Children's achievement can be assessed in either a formal or an informal way.

3. Search music lesson plan
   - Search for lessons. For example:
     - You can find music lessons in activity-based books
     - You can search on websites
     - My search:

   - Modify for your practice.
     - Check if the contents of the lesson are appropriate for your lesson
     - Edit parts (if needed)
     - Adopt the procedure to be appropriate for your teaching environment

11-2. Developing Skills
11-2-(2) Daily Music

Activity 11-2-(2)

1. Find if music can be used or taught in a daily schedule.
   - Describe a typical schedule of an early childhood education program. A preschool schedule, for example[1]:
     - Opening activities
     - Group meeting/planning
     - Learning centers
     - Bathroom/hand washing
     - Snacks
     - Outdoor activity/play/walking
     - Bathroom/Toileting
     - Lunch
     - Relaxation
     - Nap time
     - Centers or special projects
     - Group time

   - Think of what kind of musical activities can be planned for a daily schedule.
     - A simple musical activity such as singing a song while children are gathering for group activity
     - Individual or group music activities children can do during free play in learning centers
     - Musical games can be used for transitional periods such as toileting
     - Rhythmic movement for relaxation
     - Music activities during group time
     - My idea:

2. Create a music lesson.
   - Develop a music lesson. Considering:
     - Musical concepts
     - Type of activities: singing, playing, dancing, creating, or listening.
     - Group type: as individual, small group, or the whole group of children.
     - Schedule: when to teach in a daily schedule
     - My lesson:

---

[1] Morrison, G. S. (2001). *Early Childhood Education Today*. 8th Edition. NJ: Merrill, Prentice Hall.

11-3. Experiencing
11-3-(1) Teaching Music

Activity 11-3-(1)

1. Teach a music lesson to a group of children.
    - Prepare for the lesson. For example:
    - Make visual aids or devices
    - Select music
    - Set up area
    - What I need to do for my lesson:

    - Teach children the lesson you've planned. Keep in mind:
    - To be flexible in time to get children's attention
    - To be interactive in questioning
    - To respect each child's pace
    - To help children at their developmental level
    - My reminder:

2. Share your feeling and thoughts after the lesson.
    - Share on your lesson
    - What worked and didn't work in your activity
    - How children responded to each part of the lesson plan
    - How you felt during each procedure
    - My feelings and thoughts:

    - Discuss how you can improve your lesson.
    - Which part of the lesson plan should be edited
    - How lesson plan can be presented better in the future
    - How it should be modified if you teach a different group of children
    - How teaching and instruction skills should be developed
    - My thought:

11-3. Experiencing
11-3-(2) Developmentally Appropriate Practice

Activity 11-3-(2)

1. Observe children's musical development
    - Observe two or three children in a classroom setting. For example:
    - How often they play in the music area
    - What they do in the music area
    - Musical behavior in other areas
    - Musical behavior or an interaction during play
    - My observation:

    - Observe two or three children during music time. For example:
    - How they respond to music
    - How the children were different from each other
    - Their understanding of musical concepts
    - Musical skills shown in music activities
    - My observation:

2. Discuss issues in teaching children
    - Children with different needs. What kind of different needs can children have? For example:
    - Types of children's needs: Gifted, learning disabilities, physically handicapped, behavioral problems, or other needs:
    - Self efficacy in teaching children with different needs
    - My thoughts and feelings:

    - Assessment
    - How do you know the activity you've planned is developmentally appropriate for the children?
    - How would you assess children's musical development?
    - My thoughts and feeling:

Reflection on Unit 11

1. At this juncture, what is your definition of:
   - Standards
   - Theory

2. What will you do to:
   - Learn about elements of a lesson plan
   - Plan music
   - Teach music and evaluate

3. My reflection on the music-related experience in Unit 11.
   - With respect to my personal learning and growth
   - In terms of my future teaching experience

Whether it is based on a standard or a theory,
prior focus should be on children's musical development.

Unit 12: Music and Technology

Technology
*

Object, process, knowledge, and volition
that extend human capabilities and the environment.

·

When appropriately integrated into curriculum,
technology can be a powerful tool
both for classroom teachers and for the children

Unit 12
Music and Technology

You will learn and reflect on music and teaching through:

12-1. Building Knowledge

12-1-(1) Technology and Music
12-1-(2) Sources Using Technology

12-2. Developing Skills

12-2-(1) Electronics for Music
12-2-(2) Computers for Music

12-3. Experiencing

12-3-(1) Technology for Children
12-3-(2) Technology for Teachers

12-1. Building Knowledge
12-1-(1) Technology and Music

Activity 12-1-(1)

1. Learn about technology.
   - Define technology.
   - Technology is objects (tools, machines), process (design and transformation of material), knowledge (know-how, technique), and volition (aims, intentions, and choices that link the other three) which extend human capabilities and environment.[1]
   - My definition:

2. Discuss the relationship between technology and music.
   - What can we consider as technology for music in a class? For example:
   - Objects: Computers, CD player, Musical instruments, etc.
   - Knowledge: How to play musical instruments
   - My thought:

   - How can technology help teachers teach children music?
   - Technology can be used as a tool in teaching as we use music players to play musical CDs for children's rhythmic movement.
   - My thought:

   - How is it useful to use technology for children in developing their musical ability and/or learning music in class? For example:
   - Children can develop music appreciation as they listen to the music played on the radio, music player, and so forth.
   - Children can create music using technology as they play melody on a keyboard.
   - My thought:

---

[1] Frey, R.. (1989). A Philosophical Framework for Understanding Technology. *Journal of Industrial Teacher Education*, 27(1), 23-35

12-1. Building Knowledge
12-1-(2) Sources Using Technology

Activity 12-1-(2)

---

1. Research videos that can be used for music-related activities, in addition to the videos made for children's music.

   - Some give information and explanation about musical concepts. For example:
     - Music Appreciation: Music... series[1]
     - Why Toes Tap[2]

   - Some give information and sounds of musical instruments from different culture. For example:
     - The JVC Video Anthology of World Music and Dance series [3]

   - Some give an idea of how we can use the objects around us to make a musical sound.
     - Stomp Outloud[4]

   - Animation or actions with music can be created.
     - Wildlife Symphony[5]
     - Fantasia[6]
     - My search:

   - Some movie clips can encourage making music. For example:
     - Movie clips with rhythmic action.
     - Movies with beautiful images such as a river flowing, falling leaves, etc.
     - My search:

---

[1] *Music Appreciation: Music...is Tone Color.* CA: Valencia Entertainment.
[2] *Marsalis on Music: Why Toes Tap*; with Seiji Ozawa. VHS. 1995. Sony Music Entertainment Inc.
[3] *The JVC Video Anthology of World Music and Dance.* Cambridge, MA: A Production of JVC, Victor Company of Japan, Ltd.
[4] *Stomp Outloud.* VHS. 1997. New York: Yes/No Productions Ltd.
[5] *Wildlife Symphony.* VHS. 1993. CA: The Reader's Digest Association, Inc.
[6] *Fantasia.* VHS. 2000. Walt Disney.

2. Research children's software for music.
    - There are different types of educational software such as[1]:
    - *Tutorials* present students with new information to be learned and provide interactive practice and feedback.
    - *Drill-and-practice* provides students with interactive practice and feedback of information for which students have already received instruction.
    - *Learning Games* provide competition with time constraints, points earned, and/or computer characters with learned material.
    - *Problem-Solving* presents students with situations that require the use of higher-order thinking skills to achieve the intended outcome(s). Many of them involve simulations of "real-world" situations and often are game-like.
    - *Process Tools* provide students with a set of tools to assist them with completing a designated process such as concept mapping, writing, graphing, or designing.

    - Examine music software for children and discuss how each of them can be educational in music. For example:
    - *Children's Songbook:* Award-winning collection of fifteen traditional musical favorites from around the world, accompanied by animated film, lyrics, musical notation, games, and information on the song and the culture that produced it.
    - *Making Music:* Award-winning composing space by drawing on screen, seeing, hearing, and learning the basics of musical composition.
    - *Sound Toys:* New way to make music through composing, recording, and saving soundscape creations.
    - *A Silly Noisy House:* Exploring sounds by manipulating objects
    - My search:

---

[1] Morrison, G. R. (2002). Chapter 14. Educational Software. p.328. In *Integrating Computer Technology into the Curriculum*. NJ: Pearson Education, Inc. Merrill Prentice Hall

3. Research music-related websites.

- You may need to download some applications to your computer to view and hear special effects on websites. For example:
  - *RealAudio* to listen to audio
  - *QuickTime* to view digital movies
  - *Shockwave* to view animations
  - *Acrobat Reader* to view portable documents

- Visit some of the sites and examine them. Print out some information you think is helpful from each site and share ideas on how you can utilize the site. For example:
  - http://www.pbskids.org helps children learn about musical concepts.
  - http://www.lehigh.edu/zoellner/encyclopedia.html gives information about popular musical instruments, playing their music, and fun learning about their origins.
  - http://www.kididdles.com/mouseum contains downloadable songs for children
  - http://www.bestchildrensmusic.com has a library of children's music
  - http://www.kids-space.org/air/air.html lets you listen to kids from around the world playing songs they wrote or playing their own instruments.
  - http://www.mamalisa.com has children's songs and lyrics from around the world
  - www.childrensmusic.org offers teaching ideas with information on books, music curricula, songs and music games.
  - http://www.snaptuit.com introduces books, activities, and recordings to help children learn music appropriate for classrooms.
  - http://www.reboprecords.com introduces award-winning CDs and cassettes for kids and grown-ups
  - http://www.musicmotion.com introduces music teaching materials, books, CDs and cassettes, videos, etc.
  - My search:

12-2. Developing Skills
12-2-(1) Electronics for Music

Activity 12-2-(1)

1. Recording and Playing
   - Discuss effective ways of using the tape/CD recorder and player for music teaching. For example:
   - You can provide a recorded tape of music, played by different musical instruments, along with picture cards to introduce musical instruments.
   - A tape/CD player can be used for children's rhythmic movement, singing, and playing of musical instruments such as percussions.
   - A tape/CD player is a useful tool to play background music in the classroom.
   - My thought:

   - Plan an activity to introduce the tape/CD recorder/player (to be used for music) to children. For example:
   - You can attach different color stickers on buttons (play, stop, and so forth depending on needs) so that children can recognize the function of each button
   - During free play, a teacher can explain how to use the recorder and player with small groups of children in the music area.
   - In circle time, a teacher can explain how the recorder and player function, giving an example and letting the children try during free play.
   - After explaining how it functions, you can record children singing and then play back so that the children can listen to what they've recorded.
   - Record a storybook with children, making musical sounds when turning a page or in certain parts of the story.
   - My idea:

2. Using a video cassette recorder (VCR)
   - Discuss how the VCR can be related to teaching music.
   - By watching videos to gain musical information
   - By playing music while watching musical movement in a video
   - My idea:

   - Plan a musical activity using the VCR. For example:
   - You can show a video that has rhythmic movement along with the music
   - Mute the sound in a certain part so that children can see pictures only. Then let them make music by using instruments or their voices.
   - Other ideas:

12-2. Developing Skills
12-2-(2) Computers for Music

Activity 12-2-(2)

1. Think about ways to use a computer in teaching music to children.
   - You can make visual materials using a computer. For example:
   - To teach a song, you can use a presentation program such as PowerPoint where you write the words of a song, draw some pictures, and so forth.
   - My idea:

   - You can use a computer in integrating music. For example:
   - Children can draw pictures while listening to different styles of music. You can scan children's drawings and make a file with music in a computer so that children can see their works while listening to music.
   - My idea:

2. Plan activities to use music software.
   - Think about an activity that children need to do before using the software. For example:
   - Children may need to learn basic concepts or skills before using the software.
   - Class rules such as how to take a turn may need to be set to use a computer.
   - My idea:

   - Think about an activity the children might be doing while using a computer. For example:
   - An interaction a child can do with other children while using music software.
   - A musical environment to encourage children's musical development while using software
   - My idea:

   - Think of some activities children can do after finished using a computer. For example:
   - Activities to check what the children have learned
   - Follow-up activities the children can do after using the software
   - My idea:

12-3. Experiencing
12-3-(1) Technology for Children

Activity 12-3-(1)

---

1. Discuss some issues that children may have with a computer in the classroom.
   - What are the advantages or disadvantages of using computers with children? For example:
   - The computer can enhance children's development such as problem-solving, non-verbal and verbal skills, long-term memory, and conceptual skills.[1]
   - It is not good to use the computer for children younger than three who learn through their bodies and need to master other skills such as crawling, walking, talking, toilet training, and so forth.[2]
   - My thought:

   - Discuss developmentally appropriate practice and technology for children. For example[3]:
   - A professional judgment by the teacher is required to determine if a specific use of technology is age appropriate, individually appropriate, and culturally appropriate.
   - Used appropriately, technology can enhance children's cognitive and social abilities.
   - Appropriate technology is integrated into the regular learning environment and used as one of many options to support children's learning
   - Early childhood educators should promote equitable access to technology for all children and their families. Children with special needs should have increased access when this is helpful.
   - The power of technology to influence children's learning and development requires that attention be paid to eliminating stereotyping of any group or eliminating exposure to violence, especially a problem-solving strategy.
   - Teachers, in collaboration with parents, should advocate for more appropriate technology applications for all children.
   - The appropriate use of technology has many implications for early childhood professional development.

---

[1] Cardelle-Elawar, M., & Wetzel, K. (1995). Students and Computers as Partners in Developing Students' Problem-Solving Skills. *Journal of Research on Computing in Education, 27*(4), 374-401.
Haugland, S. W., & Wright, J. L. (1992). The Effect of Computer Software on Preschool Children's Developmental Gains. *Journal of Computing in Childhood Education*, 3(1), 15-30

[2] Elkind, D. (1998). Computers for Infants and Young Children. *Child Care Information Exchange*, 123, 44-46.

[3] National Association for the Education of Young Children. (1996). NAEYC Position Statement: Technology and Young Children- Ages Three Through Eight. *Young Children*, 51(6), 11-16. http://www.naeyc.org/resources/position_statements/pstech98.htm

2. Discuss some issues involving children using CD-ROM/software.
    - What are some concerns or benefits with the use of software for children? For example:
        - Depending on the quality of the software and how to make a connection, children can increase/decrease learning. For instance, in traditional ways, children will only use drills in basic skills and instructional games.[1]
        - Good software may enhance children's development such as reading comprehension.[2]
        - My thought:

    - What criteria should we use in selecting software for children? For example[3]:
        - Accuracy: information is correct and consistent.
        - Effective instructional strategies: learners, maintaining interest, control various program features and get an appropriate feedback.
        - Meets instructional objectives.
        - Easy of use in directions with technical quality.

    - How can we apply the criteria above in selecting music software for children? For example:
        - Accuracy: the software should have correct information about musical concepts.
        - Effective instructional strategies: learners should be able to maintain interest on music while controlling program features.
        - Meets instructional objectives of music.

    - Review children's software.
        - http://www.superkids.com/
        - http://www/childrenssoftware.com/
        - My review:

---

[1] Healy, J. M. (1998). *Failure to Connect: How Computers Affect Our Children's Minds-For Better and Worse*. New York: Simon & Schuster.
[2] Matthews, K. (1997). A Comparison of the Influence of Interactive CD-ROM Storybooks and Traditional Print Storybooks on Reading Comprehension. *Journal of Computing in Education*, 29(3), 263-73.
[3] Gill, B. J., Dick, W., Reiser, R. A., & Zahner, J. E. (1992). A New Model for Evaluating Instructional Software. *Educational Technology*, 32(3), 39-44.
  Hannafin, M. J., & Peck, K. L. (1998). *The Design, Development, and Evaluation of Instructional Software*. New York: Macmillan Publishing Co.
  Reiser, R. A., & Dick, W. (1990). Evaluating Instructional Software. *Educational Technology Research and Development,* 38(3), 43-50

12-3. Experiencing
12-3-(2) Technology for Teachers

Activity 12-3-(2)

1. Discuss some issues on the use of the Internet for teaching methods.
    - Why do we need to use technology such as the Internet in contemporary education? For example:
      - The population of Internet users is growing[1]
      - My thoughts:

    - What are some benefits of the Internet in teaching music? For example:
      - The Internet can make education more attainable and promote improved and new types of learning.[2]
      - Teachers can easily get musical information such as musical pieces, knowledge of music theory, ideas of teaching music, music materials, etc.
      - My thought:

2. Share how you feel about using a computer.
    - What computer skills do you have? For example:
      - Word processing, PowerPoint presentation, MIDI, etc.
      - My skills:

    - Think about how computer skills can be used in teaching music to children.
      - I might use:

    - Are you confident in using the computer in your class?
      - My feeling and/or concerns:

    - How do you think you can resolve the concerns and improve your computer skills?

---

[1] Morrison, G. R. (2002). *Integrating Computer Technology into the Curriculum.* NJ: Pearson Education, Inc. Merrill Prentice Hall
[2] Owston, R. D. (1997). The WWW: A Technology to Enhance Teaching and Learning? *Educational Researcher*, 26(2), 27-33.

Reflection on Unit 12

1. At this juncture, what is your personal definition of:
   - Technology

2. What activities will you use in the classroom to:
   - Use musical sources of technology
   - Plan and teach music using technology

3. My reflection on the music-related experience in Unit 12.
   - With respect to my personal learning and growth
   - In terms of my future teaching experience

Technology can be a powerful tool,
both for classroom teachers and for children.
The classroom teacher takes the key role
in evaluating appropriate uses of technology,
integrating technology into the typical learning environment.